About the Author

Dianne Sylvan has been Wiccan for ten years and holds a second degree in the Sibylline Order of Wicca. She is an ordained minister with an earnest desire to see other Wiccans embrace their spirituality as a living, vibrant path.

To Write to the Author

If you wish to contact the author or would like more information about this book, please write to the author in care of Llewellyn Worldwide and we will forward your request. Both the author and publisher appreciate hearing from you and learning of your enjoyment of this book and how it has helped you. Llewellyn Worldwide cannot guarantee that every letter written to the author can be answered, but all will be forwarded. Please write to:

Dianne Sylvan
℅ Llewellyn Worldwide
P.O. Box 64383, Dept. 0-7387-0348-6
St. Paul, MN 55164-0383, U.S.A.

Please enclose a self-addressed stamped envelope for reply,
or $1.00 to cover costs. If outside U.S.A., enclose
international postal reply coupon.

Many of Llewellyn's authors have websites with additional information and resources. For more information, please visit our website at http://www.llewellyn.com.

The Circle Within

Creating
a
WICCAN
Spiritual
Tradition

DIANNE SYLVAN

2003
Llewellyn Publications
St. Paul, Minnesota 55164-0383, U.S.A.

First Edition
First Printing, 2003

Book design and editing by Joanna Willis
Cover art © 2002 by PhotoDisc
Cover design by Lisa Novak

Library of Congress Cataloging-in-Publication Data
Sylvan, Dianne, 1977–
   The circle within: creating a wiccan spiritual tradition / Dianne
Sylvan.—1st ed.
      p.   cm.
   Includes bibliographical references and index.
   ISBN 0-7387-0348-6
      1. Witchcraft. 2. Spiritual life. I. Title.

BF1566.S95 2003
299—dc21

                                                      2003047663

Llewellyn Publications
A Division of Llewellyn Worldwide, Ltd.
P.O. Box 64383, Dept. 0-7387-0348-6
St. Paul, MN 55164-0383, U.S.A.
www.llewellyn.com

Printed in the United States of America

Contents

Contents

Acknowledgments

I give thanks to the God and Goddess, who gave me a heart, mind, breath, words, and hands.

I thank every man and woman who has ever raised an athame in greeting to the full moon, and those who walk the Path with grace and honor.

I am grateful to the teachers and friends, priestesses and sacred clowns, students and ghosts of good humor I am lucky to know: my family, Shana, Jim, Amber, Kimberley, Amy, Sarah, Ryan, Jess, Laura, Kathy, Paul, Sybil, Bill, Peggy, Laurie, Daniel, the Sibylline Order, and the entire Tribe of Ancient Ways.

Lastly, I give thanks to Scott Cunningham, whose words led me to the Circle.

Preface

I came to Wicca without the benefit of a human teacher. I grew up in small-town Texas in a predominantly Catholic rural area in a Baptist household. There was no Internet then, and if there were any secret Wiccan groups around, I certainly was not privileged to know them. For the first two years of my practice I had no tools, no candles, no incense, or robes—only my heart, reason, and Scott Cunningham's *Wicca: A Guide for the Solitary Practitioner* (hidden between my mattress and box spring).

For all the loneliness inherent in that sort of path, I don't regret a minute of it. During that time I talked to the God and Goddess a lot, and They answered. Most often the Goddess sent Her messages in the form of the local birds of prey. Red-tailed hawks and white barn owls had a way of showing up at convenient times in those first years, just when I needed encouragement. I found in Wicca a beauty and nurturing that came from the trees and fields of my homeland, and from the whispers of the Divine among the swaying rows of maize. It was years before I realized there were people who didn't feel the same way about their spirituality as I did, and that realization came as a bit of a shock. I saw a lot of unhappy people who put on robes and "played witch" eight times a year, or any time there was a festival with free-flowing mead. I saw adults acting like bratty children, gossiping and fighting amongst themselves about things like degrees and titles that meant absolutely nothing outside their particular group. I saw Wiccans who were as divorced from Spirit as many Christians I knew, and it saddened me.

Fortunately, I also met many wonderful people, great teachers, and friends who derive the same happiness from Wicca that I do. After being in the community for a few years, I came to the conclusion that if I could have one wish for all of us, it would be to help other people find the same day-to-day joy, wonder, and fulfillment that the love of God and Goddess has brought me.

Around the time I made that conclusion, Spider stepped in.

I am not overwhelmingly psychic; I don't hear voices, see auras, astral project, or any of the other worthy pursuits a lot of my contemporaries engage in. I feel they're all perfectly valid, just not necessary for me. I carry on conversations with trees and stones and sometimes with houses, but my magic has always worked perfectly well without belaboring the difference between alpha and beta states. However, I do know when Someone is trying to tell me something, if only because messages from the Divine generally come to me as the psychic equivalent of being hit from behind with a balloon full of gravel. I knew that the Goddess followed me with feathers in the beginning, and that I could trust Her creatures as messengers.

So, when all of a sudden I started seeing spiders everywhere, I knew it was no coincidence. For one thing, I think spiders are icky and I don't go out of my way to come across them. For another, in Texas we are blessed with some of the deadlier spiders known to humankind, so I learned from childhood not to get too close to our eight-legged sisters. That means that when one crawled out of my shoe one morning, I automatically shrieked and whacked it with *Webster's New Collegiate Dictionary*.

After a few weeks of whacking left and right, I thought something must be up. The spiders weren't just appearing in reality, there were images of webs everywhere I went—from business icons to broken truck windows—and they haunted my dreams in a very nonthreatening but impatient way. I began to feel like the victim of a cosmic and private joke. That was when I looked up spiders in several books on animal symbolism, and realized what they were telling me.

"We are the recordkeepers," they said. "We weave a sacred trust; the path of Spirit lies in the heart of our web. We weave with silk, and you weave with words. Pick up the threads and make an offering. Hey, are you listening? Get off your rump and write your book!"

As illuminating as that was, it wasn't a particularly new idea. I've been writing stories and poetry since I was four, and I always knew if I were to be happy in this world, I would have to write. I'd also been in a creative slump since graduating from high school, when the "real world" got in the way of my fantasies. Write a book? Sure. But which one?

That very night, I had a rather hilarious dream. I dreamed I was sitting on my couch eating ice cream and watching a Monty Python movie when suddenly my living room began to sprout. Flowers grew from the television, vines dropped from the ceiling, and in half a minute the whole room was an ocean of green. My cat, in the dream, was not amused.

Then a spider about a foot wide lowered herself from what was my ceiling fan, looked at me, and said, "You are human, and especially dense, so we're making it easier on you. It's been in your mind for years, you know; you just never had the courage or drive to make it real. Here's what you must do . . ." (That's not an exact quotation, but you get the idea.)

Simple as that, this book was born.

Most of the people who have heard that story nodded and said something to the effect of, "So have you started writing yet?" Of course, most of those people were Pagans. I did tell one woman at my office, who recommended that I "lay off the drugs."

Regardless, from the knotted and frayed threads of my web, I offer you this book.

Introduction

This is not a book on beginning Wicca. I feel there are plenty of wonderful (and not so wonderful) books out there for complete novices, and you'll find a few at the end of this book in the recommended reading section. The basics of Wicca really are not that complicated, and if you can't get what you need to start off from those myriad books, I don't think I can help you. This book assumes you are far along enough that I don't need a glossary with words like *athame*.

This is not a book of spells. In fact, you will not find a single spell in these pages. Why not? Again, I think there are way more than enough books of spells out there. I am writing from a purely spiritual perspective, and my goal is to help Wiccans become closer to the God and Goddess, not win them a mate or a new car. To me, making magic is a religious act that must be considered in the context of our relationship with Deity, and that relationship needs more attention than the props and symbols involved in spellcasting.

I have also recommended some ethical, practical books on spells and their casting later on. I mean, let's face it: many Wiccans came to this path because of the idea of spellwork and the thought of being able to exert some control over the crazy turns of their lives. Despite what popular culture would have us believe, *Wicca* and *spellcraft* are not synonyms, and Wicca is not something quirky to do to amaze your friends or piss off your family. It's a shame that with so much emphasis these days on getting what we want, we forget to acknowledge the mystery of Divine love and compassion. This mystery is the focus of this book.

So what does this book have to offer?

It is, at heart, a guide to creating your own spiritual practice based on the idea that every act can be a ritual, and that every moment we are alive is another chance to honor the Divine within and around us. The techniques offered here are guideposts; a way of helping you discover how you can best express yourself spiritually. This is not holy writ; I make no claims to superiority or guru-hood. I am only a Wiccan, and that is everything I strive to be. Feel free to pick and choose, improvise, and alter whatever makes you the most comfortable and whatever helps you on your personal path.

This book hinges on the idea that all ethical paths are right ones. The path I am describing is adaptable to any tradition; the connection with the Divine is the focus, not the vocabulary words. I don't care what the names or origins of your gods are, where you place your altar, what color your robe is, or how many degrees you have garnered. I don't care if your pantheon is based on Tolkien novels or if you are an anarchist-faery-vegetarian-Klingon Wiccan. What matters to me is what's in your heart, how you feel about your faith, and that you live your religion as ethically and honestly as possible.

This book is divided into two parts. The first part details the underlying concepts and practices that form the backbone of creating a spiritual practice. Here you will find tools to help you fashion your personal tradition. Chapters 1 through 7 will cover the foundations of our spiritual lives, such as our relationship with Deity, concepts of sacred space, ethics, and views of the Wheel of the Year and creating ritual. Part two, "The Book of Moonlight," is a sort of devotional Book of Shadows, giving examples of prayers, meditations, and rituals you might incorporate into your version of Wicca.

The rituals and suggestions here come from a very eclectic, hearth-based tradition that does not adhere to any particular pantheon or culture. My tradition considers the home as sacred space, and our everyday actions to be as holy as the longest scripted ritual ever produced by the Grand Order of High Mucketymucks. My personal practice blends basic Wiccan tenets with a little Zen, a little kitchen witchery, a bit of Druidry, and a generous helping of humor.

As I look out my window I can see the moon in all her radiant glory, and my heart constricts with joy that there are such wonders in the world and I am here to see them all. I hope that reading this book will give you a glimpse into that joy, and help you to find your own. If it does, I have done more in this life than I ever thought I could.

Blessed be.

PART ONE

one

Stepping into the Circle

THE GODDESS IS ALIVE AND well in Texas.

Her sacred grove is a one-bedroom apartment on the East Side, where the traffic noise rattles the windows and rain leaks in through the crack above the door. In the age of computers and stock portfolios, She has traded Her celestial raiment for a business suit. The Hands that spun the web of creation chop vegetables, light incense, type letters. The Voice that called the stars into being answers the hotline at the domestic violence shelter downtown. The Goddess sings Aretha Franklin in the shower at night, and sometimes She forgets who She is.

Then She looks in the mirror and sees the light of the Sacred in Her eyes. She remembers dancing bare-breasted at Beltane and standing with arms upraised in the center of a ring of oaks with chant ringing in Her ears as She weighs dragon's blood resin at the local metaphysical supply store. She thinks of the praise that falls from Her lips on a moonlit night. She remembers Herself.

So can you.

By now you have read books on Wicca, searched the Internet like a big-game hunter on safari, and networked until you couldn't tell one Amber or Raven from another. You've bought specially charged candles and been to festivals; you've memorized lists of correspondences for colors, days of the week, elements, astrological signs, herbs, deities, and animals. Maybe you have been part of a coven or other sort of group, maybe not. You have certainly gathered quite a collection of ritual robes, jewelry, and tubes of henna paste.

The problem, however, is not with whom you have worked or what you have worn. The problem is that you look in the mirror and you still don't remember who you are. Life feels heavy, and the rituals you attend have started to bore you. There is something fundamental that's missing from your religion, and you hate to admit it. After all, when you found Wicca, it felt so much like coming home. Does your dissatisfaction mean you're in the wrong house after all this time?

Before you start to pack, consider this: humans are a species constantly in search. At the beginning of our history we searched for food, and when we realized that potential food was much bigger than we were, we searched for a big stick to hit it with. We searched for shelter, and then when the basic issues of survival were covered, we searched for community so we wouldn't have to face the dark nights alone. Once we learned to band together and share the labor, we had time to search for something bigger: meaning, purpose, something to explain why we are here and why we share our existence with disagreeable things like murder, flood, politicians, and mosquitoes. We needed something to give us a place in the universe—a vantage point from which things made sense.

Religion of any kind is a way to find that something. It became clear to the human race that the meaning of life—the purpose of it all—would not be the same for every person. Hence the rise of so many religions and philosophies. Every faith approaches the search in a different way and finds a different idea to focus on. Christians, most often, seek salvation from our own sinful natures and deliverance from the evils of the world. Put very simply, Buddhists seek enlightenment—a transcendence of the physical realm in order to pursue the spiritual one. Wiccans, along with a number of others, seek union.

Someone once asked me, "What's the point of this Wicca thing? I mean, if you're not trying to get into Heaven or find Nirvana, what are you trying to do?"

That is a tough one, and a question I don't think many of us have given a lot of thought to. It is difficult to step back and look at the bigger picture. I gave the only answer I knew, then or now. The point of Wicca, the real mystery behind it all, is to remember the Divinity within ourselves and all things; to manifest our God and Goddess all the time, every day, every moment; to love as They love, to give as They give; to serve Them in perfect trust, and thus bring Their grace more fully into the world; to understand that we are the embodiment of the Divine love and nurture, and to express that love in the world; to walk as God and Goddess.

Sound impossible? It isn't. We already have all the tools we need; we only have to recognize them and teach ourselves how to use them to return to a view of the world where anything is possible—to see like a child with wide eyes and an open heart.

The rituals and other tools of Wicca serve as a bridge between ourselves and that goal, and as tools they can be used effectively or clumsily. I can't count the number of rituals I have attended where the most spiritual part of the event was the potluck afterward when everyone shook off the boredom of another full moon just like the hundred before it and really got to celebrate. The most moving rituals are the ones with the fewest stage directions and the least fuss, where energy flows along its natural currents and we dance with it. Unfortunately these are in the minority for most groups, and in solo Wicca it can be even harder to create a sense of the sacred when using the same old chants and the same old colored candles. We try not to venture too far from what we've learned from books and covenmeets, since branching out means that eventually our branches will intersect with those of other religions. Wiccans have great pride, I have noticed, in how different we are from the world's biggest sects. Perhaps we think it shows growth on our part, or perhaps we simply want to distance ourselves from the ways of our youth that often left us scarred and wanting. We forget the moments of fellowship, the hymns that were part of our blood, the parts of ourselves that those faiths actually did satisfy even if we grew beyond them and went searching for something more.

The problem is that in our desire to separate ourselves from our childhood faiths and eke out a place of our own in the grand scheme of things, we refuse to learn from our religious heritage. Obviously if the Christians do it, it must be useless. Never mind the millions of people who do find the Christian tradition a fulfilling path. Never mind the people out there who are striving to be *Christlike*—not political, who are not our enemies. We can't learn anything from them, of course. Everything we need as Wiccans is in a book somewhere or in ourselves or in the natural world, right?

The vast majority of our co-religionists nowadays have read all the books on beginning Wicca they can stomach and don't live anywhere near the natural world that our ancestors had to struggle with for daily survival. It's difficult to revere nature with any sense of reality when the nearest natural area is thirty miles away and the closest thing to it is a manufactured park littered with beer cans and stray drug dealers. We spend all day encased in metal and glass, going from house to car to office and back again, and many even work through meals.

Where does that leave us? We are in many ways disconnected from the nature we are supposed to worship. If having a ritual outdoors means schlepping into the country with a ten-pound bag of ritual tools (the mystical Tote Bag of Shadows) and soaking ourselves in bug repellant, what do we do the other three hundred or so days of the year? In our society we are constantly bombarded with images of violence, hatred, and indifference, and our attempts to change things are often met with hostility. The magic in the world sometimes seems to have a precarious hold on life at best. How can you live as a

Wiccan every day when your lifestyle is better suited to urban guerilla warfare?

It isn't enough to be a Wiccan on full moons or sabbats. No one ever became fluent in a new language by using it once a month. The best way is to surround yourself with the lesson; to speak Wiccan from dawn to dusk until it becomes your nature.

One oft-overlooked remedy for our modern dilemma is the ancient tradition of a daily personal practice. In every religion the world over there are people who take the devotional path, giving over large parts of their day to ritual, prayer, and communion with whatever face God wears for them. The dictionary definition of the word *devotion* is to give wholeheartedly to something. Given the Wiccan view of the universe as a place of cause and effect, it would follow that the more you devote to your sense of the Divine, the more the Divine will devote to you. If our goal as Wiccans is to turn our belief in the God and Goddess into reality, immersing ourselves in our relationship with Them is the surest way to turn our belief into knowledge.

How do I know this? My life is every bit as hectic and the city I live in every bit as toxic as most people's. I haven't reached some blissful state of spiritual perfection, but I have seen its nearest neighbor in people I have encountered over the years, and I have begun to learn from their success.

The first group I noticed whose religion and life were as one were Catholic nuns who worked in the hospital where I was a secretary at the age of twenty-two. There were several elderly Sisters who tended to the patients' spiritual needs, and in a building full of trauma and pain they were always calm, gracious, and quick to smile. They moved with quiet surety through the halls, their voices gentle and almost musical. Speaking to any of the Sisters gave my spirits a lift, which was vital given how much I hated the job.

I had to wonder, though, what got them through? They saw the worst of humanity in an endless parade of communicable diseases and gunshot wounds, yet maintained their sense of grace. I had to know if they could still smile when they got home at night, or if it took all their strength just to stay human in such a place.

Finally I asked one of the nuns how she dealt with such a stressful workplace. She smiled at me rather beatifically and told me that when she got up in the morning she prayed. At breakfast, lunch, and dinner she prayed. At bedtime she prayed, and a dozen other moments in between, keeping in constant, loving dialogue with God. The nuns didn't just believe the tenets of their faith, they lived them from morning till night.

I couldn't help but be impressed, as well as feel a little sheepish. I had tried for a long time to tell myself that there was nothing that I could learn from Christians; that their narrow-mindedness was the reason the world was going to their hell in a handbasket. In other words, I'd been as narrow as I thought they were. It was what some of my Pagan contemporaries call a "cosmic two-by-four"—a whop in the head from the gods when you've been an idiot.

The idea of daily practice, however, stuck with me long after I had taken the lesson of tolerance to heart. I started to

ask around among my Pagan friends, finding out to my cha-
grin that, for the most part, they were bereft of any sort of
personal daily rituals beyond a few minutes of meditation.
Life was simply too busy, they said, to do half the things they
wanted to to stay in touch with the God and Goddess.

That led me to wonder whether a life too busy for our
deepest beliefs is really much of a life at all.

After hunting down a number of books on the monastic
life, I discovered that in the arena of personal practice, the
humble monks and nuns had us beat. Naturally it's easier to
devote your entire life to God if you live in an abbey, where
the environment exists to support your religious quest. Yet
despite the inherent differences between monastic and lay
lives, there are valuable lessons to be found from these little
communities, regardless of creed or location.

Buddhist monks—and, indeed, a great number of Buddhists in the larger world—have similar practices to the
Catholics. They move in a rhythm of mindfulness and meditation throughout the day, even using housework as an opportunity to meditate on the wonder of the present moment. To a
Buddhist, every action is a chance to learn and grow spiritually. As a result, the Buddhist reaches a state of emotional
equilibrium where stress and angst have only a fleeting place
in the course of the day.

The Sufi dervishes, who practice a form of Islamic mysti-
cism, integrate their prayer and liturgy with dance, music,
and the well-known "whirling" that helps the practitioner
reach Allah. The poet Rumi, credited with founding Sufism
as a sect, frequently referred to God as "the Beloved."

Meanwhile, Westerners run around with cellular phones plastered to their heads shrieking at each other in traffic and having heart attacks on an alarmingly regular basis.

Hmm.

Even among laypeople, Christians and Jews appear to have an easier time integrating their spiritual lives with their daily ones, perhaps because so many people have given it so much thought. Those who *want* to become more spiritually attuned in mainstream religions have dozens of resources at their fingertips.

Take, for example, the recent "What Would Jesus Do?" phenomenon. It may seem like more of a marketing ploy than a religious precept, but if you look past the merchandise and into a less cynical view, it is an excellent way to integrate faith and the mundane world. Taken at face value it is a profound question. How would a deity act in this situation? What would he say? Are my own actions following my religious ideal?

Books abound on Christian and Jewish daily prayer; there are plenty of devotionals, calendars, and classes on living a prayerful life. In this way, Pagans are at a decided disadvantage. Perhaps we simply haven't given it enough thought. We learn from the outset that we are not separate from Deity, that the whole world is God and Goddess, but what do we do with that belief? How does that belief translate into direct experience in day-to-day life?

I have known a handful of Wiccans who managed to develop an integrated magical/mundane existence, and the effect is amazing. These are the truly powerful Wiccans, the ones whose every word resonates with Divinity. Their lives run more smoothly, more peacefully, and when disaster strikes, it seems to flow through them like water. The source? Daily practice, a devotional life.

Why don't more people live that way? The first cry is, "I don't have time! I have to get to my meeting and take the kids to soccer practice and answer my e-mail and get that proposal ready for Monday and clean the bathroom and wash the car and figure out what to have for dinner!"

You'd rather be doing all that than a ritual?

As a society, we have given time the power of a god. The clock is our idol and we bow to its whims, always running a little behind like the terrible sinners we are. How many minutes of the day can the average person give up without compromise? Very few, but the truth is, there is no such thing as a spiritual life without sacrifice. In the olden days perhaps it was part of the harvest or an animal (or even a member of the tribe in extreme cases) that went to the gods to show them how much they were loved and respected (and, in some cases, feared). In our time, the sacrifice must be time. We are always called by the gods to give up what we think is precious. In our day, we crave an extra two or three hours even though we waste large amounts of the extant twenty-four trying to climb the corporate ladder. Meanwhile, our inner lives languish. To find peace in the valley of the shadow, it's worth getting up twenty minutes earlier. Trust me on this one.

I find it a bit novel, and rather laughable, that a lot of Wiccans (especially the young) want their religion to serve them as quickly and efficiently as possible with a minimum of personal investment. This, actually, is true of almost everyone in the modern West. When has learning and growth ever come without a sacrifice of time? We are willing to spend years in medical school to become doctors, but want to be priestesses of the Divine *right away*.

You could view daily spiritual practice, then, as being in class working toward your degree. The difference, of course, is that rather than walking across a stage to receive a diploma as the fruit of your labors, the rewards are constantly unfolding before you, drawing you closer and closer to the God and Goddess with each turn of the Wheel of the Year.

Most monastic communities, regardless of religious affiliation, follow a set of practices and guidelines known as a "rule." In Christian monasteries the rule is usually written, and in many cases was penned hundreds of years ago by saints such as Francis or Benedict. The Rule of St. Benedict, for example, outlines the time of day for the Holy Offices and what prayers should be said when. Buddhist and other sects don't generally write the rule out so succinctly. There are also many rules that have been either created or adapted from older ones to meet the needs of modern communities.

Although these rules were designed for monks and nuns, the idea of a rule of life is a good one. It is basically the equivalent of a personal daily practice to a Wiccan. Instead of yellowed parchment with directions from clerics we've never met, we have our hearts and the beauty of the Earth and the whisper of the Goddess in our ears. We need only to codify these things, decide what is important to our spiritual growth, and lay the stones of the path as we walk on it.

This book is a sort of manual on how to start a personal practice of your own, with the goal of Divine union as a beacon. The path I am describing here is, in essence, a way of treating our religion as, well, a *religion*, twenty-four hours a day. Through daily practice and constant mindfulness of the deep connections between us and all that lives, you can find a way to reach up and take the hand you are offered. By making every act an act of reverence, you can touch something long hidden in yourself. As it stretches sleepy arms and blinks its eyes, you will find the union you so desperately craved.

It is possible. The first step is to come to the understanding—if you haven't already—that there is no distinction between the spiritual and the mundane except the one we draw ourselves. If we believe that the gods are manifest in the world, then not only is everything sacred, but every *action* is sacred. All the rituals and prayers we attach to our actions are merely ways to remind ourselves, to bring our awareness to that sanctity that was already there, waiting for us to see it.

This is not worship—at least, not in the modern sense of throwing yourself at your Deity's feet and begging for forgiveness. (I doubt They would give it to you before you had given it to yourself, anyway.) The word *worship* has such negative connotations for most NeoPagans that we might as well throw it out for our purposes. As I've said, to devote something is to give wholeheartedly. If you give the Lord and Lady your love, your time, and your energy, by nature of Wiccan precept, you will receive Theirs threefold; more often it's more like a thousandfold.

Our relationship with the gods must be one of give and take, not just take. This is a common mistake I see among pop Wiccans: cast the spell, invoke whoever you feel roughly corresponds to what you want, and *poof!* the Goddess will hand down Her miracles like a fairy godmother. To me, this is a symptom of one of the modern diseases of conscience, particularly in the West—a concept of dominion and self-centeredness whereby I am the axis the universe tilts upon and whoever has the biggest reality wins.

The Wicca you will find in these pages is a far cry from the traditions that view the gods as magical tools. Magic—or at least spellcasting—is given very little attention in my own life, but I'll share a secret with you right here and now: if you live a magical life, one filled with spirit and in contact with Divinity, you won't *need* so many spells. Think of the people you know who seem to really have it together in the religious department. They may have their fair share of misfortune, but they are better equipped to handle it without having to break out the Big Book of Badass Mojo. Wicca is a part of who they are, not just something they do eight times a year or once in the month. Magic fills their lives from head to toe to pinkie finger.

When you have learned to walk with the Divine, you begin to see things a little differently than those who treat the universe as a shopping mall. I am but a tiny thread in an infinite web of shimmering life, no more or less than the rocks and stars. I am miniscule, a blip on the radar screen—but at the same time, I am the only one of me. Each thing that takes part in living takes part in creation, and no contribution is insignificant. The slightest movement, a gentle word to one in need or a fist raised in anger, can transform worlds. We are all one, and each one in billions, and we are all made up of the love and energy of the God and Goddess.

As one of my teachers told me, "It's not enough to talk about it; the poetry isn't enough. You have to *live* it." It is the practical day-to-day action that brings it all home, making devotion a path and not simply an idea. That action is the primary focus of the following chapters.

THREE THINGS TO THINK ON

1. Up to this point, how have you seen the God and Goddess? Do They have faces and names? Are They a presence without words?

2. How much thought have you given to your personal path and why do you do things the way you do? Have you been running purely on instinct, following books by the letter, or a combination of the two? Does your altar face east for a particular reason, or because a book said it should?

3. Take a moment, or even a few days, to make a list of all the things you do in your life that make you feel spiritually fulfilled. This doesn't only include things that are viewed as traditionally spiritual, like ritual and prayer. It can be anything from playing with your children to reading,

painting, gardening, dancing, or writing if it makes you feel closer to your gods. Think of your list as your current spiritual practice, and look over it. Where are the empty spots? What sort of activities would you like to add more of? Don't make any decisions, or judgments; just think on it for a while.

two

In Search of a Mystery

"WHAT DO YOU SEE WHEN *you see Me?*" *the Goddess asked.*

I looked. "I see a woman with long dark hair, deep blue eyes that reflect the moon, strong shoulders, and capable hands. I see a serene face . . . almost always smiling."

"Look again, child."

I looked, and suddenly I was whirling out to the edges of the universe, then back, aware of every star, every planet, each creature on the Earth. I knew the pain of a billion births, the joy of a billion spring afternoons, the sound of every breath ever drawn.

"I see . . ." I stammered, still lost in the vision, "I see everything, my Lady."

"Look again."

All grew still around me, and again I looked into a woman's face. "I see gray-blue eyes, reddish hair, a small mouth. . . . Oh . . . I see myself."

She smiled. "You're learning."

As long as humans have had a concept of the world, we've had a concept of Deity. Our species looked around at the beauty and terror of our lives and felt that life was no accident, that there had to be a guiding hand to it all; otherwise, what was the point of living? Even an unkind God is better than none at all, most of us seemed to feel. There had to be a name for the strange swelling in our hearts when we saw a sunset, and for the fear that inspired us to hide from lightning.

With so many people on such a large planet with such incredible imaginations, it was inevitable that we would come up with hundreds of names for the forces that made things work. It was, I suppose, also inevitable that we argue over which names were the right ones.

When put that way it all sounds a bit silly ("My name's better than your name!"), but disputes over the nature of the gods have caused more death and suffering than any natural phenomenon.

Why?

There is nothing more personal or more deeply ingrained than the spiritual impulse in humanity. It's one of the most important parts of who we are; one of the things that supposedly separates us from the animals (although I'd bet cats have us whipped, spiritually speaking). It's also impossible to back up with clear factual evidence. How can anyone prove which gods are the true ones? You can't, and no amount of scripture-quoting or hate-mongering will bring someone around to your beliefs. At heart, the only way someone can change religion is to have a life-altering experience of another way of being, another face for the Divine. Saying you'll convert and actually converting are two entirely different things.

That, I feel, is how the Goddess survived centuries of history and hatred. You can threaten a village wise woman with death and torture and she may say "Jesus is Lord" to survive, but you can never know what's really in her heart.

I do not believe the wishful thinking that there was an underground Goddess cult that outlived and outsmarted the Christians for all those years. It's a nice idea, but there is just not much evidence to support it. However, the love of the Goddess and our need for Her doesn't require liturgy and ritual to continue. She lives in our very cells, in the yearning for love and healing and the feminine, and all the hate in the world couldn't kill Her. She simply bided Her time until we were ready for Her to return.

But who is the Goddess? Or what? And what of the God? Just whom are we calling on when we're in Circle, wreathed in incense smoke, our hearts filled with a longing that we can't name? What do Wiccans *believe* in?

Nothing.

Bet that one caught you off guard.

In order to understand the nature of Wiccan Divinity as distinct from what we grew up with (or didn't, in rare cases), we have to explore the nature of the Divine in a wider perspective. Religious scholars have developed two basic models of gods and goddesses that can be applied to just about any culture or mythos, but I propose a third, one that has characteristics of the two but is still in a way unique.

The Nature of Deity

The first model is the one that modern Christians are most accustomed to—that of *transcendent* Divinity. A transcendent god exists purely outside the world on some heavenly or astral plane. The universe is his puppet show, and he pulls the strings of the marionettes from somewhere far away. A transcendent god is unreachable, faceless, and so huge that our relationship with him is almost always one of awe, fear, and distance. Everything that happens, regardless of how horrible or wonderful, is ascribed to the "will of God," and he has a plan that we humans are not privileged to understand. Also, we cannot truly know this kind of god, as he only communicates with us through the chosen few, or in the occasional miracle such as a burning bush. Transcendence is the ultimate "I Am that I Am." (Oddly enough, this gives me a strange mental image of Jehovah as a cross between Charlton Heston and Popeye.)

The second model is known as *immanent* Divinity, and it is the one that most Wiccans prefer. An immanent deity has a distinct form, whether human or animal, and exists in the world rather than outside it. The Greek pantheon, for example, is rife with immanence. The Greek gods love, hate, have petty rivalries and grand schemes—in other words, they have *lives*. In a purely immanent pantheon, humans are often viewed as incidental to the intrigues of the gods, and we can be swept up into their dramas whether we will or no. Zeus was known for His dalliances with human women, which the women were generally less than enthusiastic about.

Some pantheons manage to combine the two models. The Hindu gods are looked on primarily as immanent, with their own lives and histories lived out in the universe. Yet at the same time, all gods are considered expressions of the greater force known as Brahman, who is essentially transcendent and unknowable. Brahman is supposedly genderless, though is usually referred to as male.

In the Christian Bible, ironically, both models of God coexist, but never at the same time. The God of Genesis creates the universe much like a sculptor with a lump of clay, and then is shown walking in the Garden of Eden and having conversations with His wayward children. Most of the time He is transcendent, thundering His orders down from the sky, but in the Book of Job He vies with Satan to see how badly He can treat a human before said human loses his faith, much in the style of Greek gods making bets and contests. Most Christian religious scholars, with the exception of those in mystical traditions, prefer the transcendent model, considering it more logical.

It would seem that in order to have a real relationship with a god, that god would almost have to be immanent. A gigantic nameless and genderless force is a bit difficult to relate to, after all. It's human nature to want our deities to look and behave as we do, so that we can come to understand them and thus ourselves.

The problem is, giving a particular name and face to a god is essentially limiting that god, penning him or her in to our own standards and making him or her smaller and less powerful. Many people balk at this idea. By naming the Goddess

Diana and the God Pan, are we taking something away from Them? In contrast, by thinking of Them as Lord and Lady without specific characteristics except male and female, are we distancing ourselves from Them? Are all those names and faces real unto themselves or are they aspects of something bigger?

In addition, it is hard to imagine a universe created by an immanent god. If there was no world before the gods, where did they come from? An immanent deity needs a place to call home, whether it's Olympus or the Garden of Eden. Only a transcendent god, existing outside our world or all around it, could fashion it out of nothing. Those who favor the approach that says the gods didn't exist until we created them, and that the universe appeared as a natural byproduct of evolution with no guiding hand, have a hard time defending their position without reducing the universe to a labyrinth of random chance where humans, once again, are supreme. Humans, after all, must be pretty powerful to create gods.

Contemporary Wiccans argue just as fiercely about these issues as people have for countless centuries, but I think the problem with such arguments is that they are based on our previous conditioning. We try to think of the God and Goddess the same way we thought of Yaweh or Allah or Jehovah, instead of rebuilding our concept of the Divine from the ground up. We forget that the Wiccan view of the universe is fundamentally different from what we grew up with, so of course our gods must be. We should therefore approach our relationship with Deity from a new direction.

Remember that in the Judeo-Christian view of the universe, God created the world as apart from Himself, with humans in His own image, and is not usually thought of as being a part of either. There is a fundamental separation in these sects between the Divine and the mortal realm, and the word of God has to be handed down through intermediaries such as priests and prophets. Even in the immanent versions of God He is still separate from us, watching us and hearing our prayers from somewhere else.

In the usual Wiccan worldview, Deity exists in everything, around everything, and as everything. Nothing is outside of or away from the Divine; everything is sacred. Deity can't be pigeonholed into *inside* or *outside* the universe; Deity *is* the universe. As such, Deity is both inside and outside; not wholly immanent, not wholly transcendent, yet more than both—*manifest*.

This is what I speak of when I say that Wiccans don't believe in anything. Nobody ever had to believe in the world—it simply *is*. We don't believe in our gods, we know them. We *are* them. Belief isn't necessary when you have direct knowledge.

The concept of manifest Deity is an intellectual contradiction. How can a god be everywhere and right here at the same time? The true nature of spirituality, however, is not intellectual. Once you have started to experience the Divine as a Wiccan, you realize that not only is the idea of manifest Deity possible, it is necessary. Only a totally new way of looking at Deity can satisfy the spirit in a world full of magic.

Deity is all things, all places, and all times, but because we are human and limited, we cannot have a full understanding of that. Therefore, we create images for our gods to inhabit, and faces and names and natures that we can grasp. The Divine force that permeates the universe can then enter into those symbols, and for us, they become real. Because the Lord and Lady love us, because They *are* love made manifest as all things, They wear whatever forms we can best relate to so that we can interact. But make no mistake: these are emblems we have created, not the totality of Goddess and God. That totality is made up of everything in the universe and its interactions, the eternal dance of probability and causality that comes from evolution, choices, love, and our lives.

Looking at Deity in this way, it's impossible to think of any other religion as "wrong." They're just different ways of arriving at the same conclusion.

What, then, is the point of all this ritual and prayer and other religious stuff?

We don't live in a world that is conducive to experiencing manifest Divinity. We are disconnected from our own sacred selves, splitting reality into the false dichotomy of mind and matter. We build ugly cities full of ugly concrete that pushes us even farther away from the sanctity of the world. We forget.

Religious practice is a way to remember. Ritual and prayer help us reforge the connection to what is sacred in the world and ourselves. We are able to step back, look around, pause, and say, "Oh yes, this is what matters." We strip off our blinders and truly see what is there.

The God and Goddess of Wicca

While the appearance of your personal God and Goddess will be unique to your own experience, Their roles in the world and in our lives are similar from one Wiccan's life to the next. That is one of the things that binds us all together as co-religionists instead of as people who use the same vocabulary merely for expediency. There are certain kinds of experiences, certain feelings about our gods that most of us seem to have in common. Generally the Lord and Lady have shared characteristics, including the following.

LOVE

The love of the God and Goddess is unconditional and without limit, which is probably the most important aspect of Their existence. Most of us are used to a God whose love is supposed to be all-pervasive, but who is also known to rage and bellow about our sins and His jealousy. Those of you who have had abusive parental relationships probably recognize that sort of fair-weather affection, and it is one of the many reasons people are flocking away from mainstream religion in this postmodern age. Why worship Someone whose love has strings attached?

The God and Goddess of Wicca, however, are not jealous or cruel. Our suffering is not Their will, imposed on us little humans for "our own good." Our own choices and our interactions with others are most often the cause of our suffering. The price of free will is risk.

Part of being a loving parent—or brother, or lover, or however you view the gods—is letting your children fall on their faces, because they have to decide for themselves when their lessons are learned. Being stubborn creatures, sometimes we have to repeat our mistakes over and over before we get the message. Though it may be painful, it's our own decision, and the Lord and Lady must stand and watch our foibles knowing that it is our free will and choice that make us who were are. A mindless automaton will never grow.

Their love, of course, includes compassion. Though They may not step in and alter the course of the universe to meet our needs or even to keep us out of harm's way, They can cushion a fall, give counsel, or soothe a broken heart. Their unwillingness to interfere in our lives is not a weakness. It is, instead, a function of integrity and nature.

The thing to remember is that although the God and Goddess are powerful beings made of the stuff of all creation, They are essentially the natural world. As such, to maintain the order of the universe, They do not often bend its rules. Everything, even the Lord and Lady, acts according to nature. That is what gives Them unshakable integrity—the integrity we strive for in our earthly existence. They are what They are, life and natural process inviolate.

BALANCE

One of my favorite names for the Goddess is "Star of Light, Abyss of Darkness." For every Bright Mother there must be a Dark Mother; for every Lord of the Living there must be one of Death. The God and Goddess encompass *all* of nature, not just the parts we like. Wiccans get a lot of flak over our tendency to ignore the darker aspects of Divinity in favor of the pretty ones. I think we do ourselves a great disservice by pretending that death and darkness are somehow less important to the cycles of life. The "white-light-and-bunny-rabbits" Wiccans are missing an entire half of what it is to live incarnate on Earth. Only by understanding the dark side of the moon can we appreciate the light and not take it for granted. Only by facing the shadows of ourselves—the nasty little hidden corners that we fear—can we be complete.

That doesn't mean we have to worship the things that hurt us. Pain doesn't ask to be worshipped, it asks only to be faced, lived through, and learned from. Life running unchecked by death is cancer, or a rainforest mowed down to raise beef cattle for an overpopulated society. Death unchecked by life is famine, plague, massacre. Neither is a natural or harmonious balance; light and dark must circle round each other in a dynamic polarity to maintain the dance of life.

Another way in which the Lord and Lady are balanced is in terms of gender. Many Wiccans make the mistake, however, of assuming there is only one way to find balance in the sexual arena: a straight God and a straight Goddess having plain old vanilla sex. While it's true that heterosexual coupling (even in a petri dish) is the only way to bring about offspring, it is most certainly not true that other kinds of pairings aren't creative as well. Any relationship that spreads more love in the world is a creative one, and therefore blessed.

I remember being in fifth grade watching a documentary on undersea life when I first got a glimpse of how rich and varied the world of sexuality could be. The camera panned across the sea floor, pausing for a moment on a pair of octopi in the middle of a tryst. The narrator informed us that not only were the two betentacled lovebirds different species, they were both male. I thought, "Now *this* is education."

The God and Goddess are all dualities, all genders, and all myriad forms of loving expression. That includes the whole rainbow spectrum from biker dykes to drag queens, hetero couples with 2.3 kids to single Mexican-American tax lawyer fetishists. As the Lady says in the Charge of the Goddess, "All acts of love and pleasure are My rituals."

SENSUALITY

While we're on the subject, the Lord and Lady differ from most other deities in modern religion in that not only do They approve of sex, They revel in it. They are sensual beings, whose dance through the seasons is grounded in the physical realm. All things that are natural to the body are holy in Their sight. Where there is love, there is blessing. Where there is coercion, violence, or fear, there is a need for healing and justice.

Wicca is a sensual religion. Our rituals are often very active, with dancing and chanting and a lot of sweat and laughter. Our magic involves all the senses: the scent of smoke, the color of candles, the sound of drums, the feeling of energy running through our bodies, the taste of sacramental wine.

Our gods are sensual as well. My first real experience with the God was in His guise as Lord of the Dance when He appeared in my living room and picked me up off the floor, saying, "Shall we?" Indeed, the universe is an erotic place where the attraction and repulsion of particles drives the most fundamental sciences. Passion in action makes the world go 'round.

LIBERATION

The service of the Lord and Lady is perfect freedom. As we become more unified with the Divine, we embrace our own power, our own liberty. We learn in Their tutelage that stepping off the beaten path frees us from the constraints of a careless society. Men are free to cry, women are free to stand up for themselves, and we are all free to love and dream.

In Their love for each other, the Goddess and God are perfect equals. In Their love for us, They are not our servants, despite what some ceremonialists believe. By the same token, They don't expect us to prostrate ourselves and beg for Their compassion. They expect us to stand and walk, to manifest Their strength and love, and to show our devotion with our lives rather than with our humiliation.

In one of the beautiful synchronicities of Wicca, I have heard several different people tell of dreams and visions of the Goddess. She came in a dozen different forms to a dozen different people, and upon seeing Her for the first time, many had the same reaction: they fell to their knees, overcome by awe.

In every one of these visions, the Goddess said, "Rise."

INSPIRATION

Few people come away from an encounter with the Divine without the sudden urge to create something, whether it's artwork, poetry, or something new of themselves. The joy we find before the Lord and Lady begs expression, and They encourage us to reach out, try new things, and find new ways to show our love for Them and thus the world.

Religious inspiration has yielded some of humankind's greatest art, literature, and music. Wiccans are certainly not immune to the desire—many of us come back to the mundane world after meeting the God and Goddess and find talents and inclinations we never knew we had. The inner priest almost always finds a voice. Some are inspired to lead or teach rather than make something. As the Lord and Lady have a thousand skills, so do Their children. Living in Their light helps us to find the confidence to explore the beauty we carry within.

Cultivating a Relationship with Deity

I can't tell you how to see the Lord and Lady. I could go on all day about how I see Them, or how traditional Wicca sees Them, but ultimately what They look like and what roles They take will depend on your inner vision and the lessons you need to learn wherever you are in your life.

I sculpt; some of my favorite things to create are little God and Goddess figures for people's altars. No matter what sort of clothes the little ones wear, however, their faces are always blank. It symbolizes to me how no two people will look into the eyes of the God and see the same thing. How our perception of the sacredness of all things manifests itself is as variable as Creation. It's one of the beautiful things about Wicca. There is a Goddess for everyone, whether tall or short or fat or transgendered or black or athletic or old or whatever. She has myriad faces, myriad tales, and only your heart and spirit will help you find the Lady for you.

No matter what faces or names we call on, however, there are ways to foster our relationship with Deity that have no boundaries. The one most Wiccans are familiar with is, of course, ritual. We create a personal temple and perform symbolic activities to connect us—or, more truthfully, to remember the connection that is already there—with Divinity.

We'll talk more about ritual in a later chapter. For now, the important thing to know is that rituals communicate with our innermost selves, the selves that speak in colors and pretty pictures and rhymes. They are a way of stepping back from our waking lives and shoring up our connection with the sacred. Then, ideally, we bring some of the wonder and love of Circle back into the daylight. If a ritual doesn't affect your daily life in some way, it wasn't effective.

One method of communication with the Divine within and without that is often overlooked, or even disdained, is prayer. I have read many books that claim spells are the Wiccan equivalent of prayer, and that since prayer is supplication and begging for favors, it should be avoided. After all, we don't bow down to our Deities, so why get on our knees and plead for help?

I disagree rather vehemently with both statements. Spells are not the same as prayers, and prayer does not have to involve begging. So what is the difference, and what makes prayer prayer?

Prayer and Magic

The kind of prayer we're brought up with is passive; a "let go and let God" where the person praying can give up ultimate responsibility for what occurs. Usually it involves saying a few halfhearted words of thanks, then goes directly into the list of complaints or requests the practitioner has compiled. Not terribly inspiring.

Prayer, in its purest form, is a formalized way of having a dialogue with your gods. It's conversation—an exchange of love and energy—most often in words but also through song, dance, art, or any creative endeavor. Prayer is any time you talk to the Goddess or God, whether to express gratitude, joy, desire, or grief. It is a way to open yourself to the Divine. It is communion, not command, and involves both speaking *and* listening.

Prayer is how we talk through our pain and problems with the Divine, and also how we tell Them how much They mean to us. In Wiccan prayer, there's nothing wrong with asking for something material, but that usually takes a back seat to expressing a feeling or asking for guidance, protection, or other things that are difficult to provide for ourselves. There comes a point when we have done all we can to keep ourselves safe and healthy and we just have to say, "Mom, Dad, anything you can do to help me out would be appreciated."

Magic is often thought of simply as "prayer with props," but I think the difference goes deeper than that. A spell is not a prayer for guidance, a quiet dialogue. It is a creative act, fusing our desire and will and vision with the Divine energy within/around us to reach a specific goal. Magic is dependent on our relationship with the Divine. As much as ceremonialists tell us that magical power is neither black nor white and can be used for anything, anyone practicing an ecstatic religion like Wicca knows that magic is inherently positive and holy.

Think of it this way: if we view the universe as a great dance, a web of probabilities and possibilities that changes with every choice we make, then magic is a way to pour our own desires into the web to shift probability toward our goals. We call upon our own Divine nature, ask for help from the elements and the Lord and Lady, and send energy into the dance to alter its course, hopefully for good.

Prayer is vital to establishing and strengthening our relationship with the God and Goddess. If you never spend any time with your family, how likely is it they'll be there when you need them? If you don't offer your time and love, can you expect anyone else's? In prayer, we set aside a moment to talk, seek guidance, give thanks. In magic, we take action, and try to assert our influence on the crazy turns of our lives. Both are important, but they're not interchangeable.

There are all types of prayer. Often the most beautiful prayers are spontaneous, like the expression of sudden joy mingled with tears when you finally reach the top of the mountain and see the world in all her bounty spread out below. There is, however, something to be said for a long-memorized and often-used prayer, like a rosary, whose words almost immediately put you in a sacred mental state and bring to mind the scent of frankincense and the sound of plainchant.

Catholics and Buddhists both use beads in their prayers, and repeat a certain phrase or verse while holding each bead, which induces a sort of trance state in which communication with the Divine flows more freely. I have used similar techniques myself, and highly recommend them, especially to someone who isn't used to prayer as a positive idea. Prayer may seem a bit odd to some Wiccans, but chanting almost certainly won't, and using prayer beads is quite similar to ritual chant.

I also recommend (and will go into greater depth in later chapters regarding) daily prayers for meals, for getting up and going to bed, and other occasions. Our lives are full of opportunities to commune with the God and Goddess. It's up to us to find them.

OPENING YOUR HEART

When you first decide to deepen your relationship with the God and Goddess, it may seem difficult to choose how to go about it. You may do a lot of rituals, say a lot of prayers, and still not feel "connected." This can be very frustrating in the beginning, since we expect to have some kind of results as soon as possible, and the voice of Deity can be almost too soft to hear.

I recommend the following exercise to start off with. Do it every morning for a month and see if you start to experience things you didn't before. The exercise is designed to help you recognize the signs and signals that the gods will send you, no matter how subtle, and to recognize Their presence in the world.

As long as your heart is open, Divine love can find you, and it will shine like a jewel. If your heart is closed, you cannot see what is essential to your spirit. The heart sees what the eyes disbelieve.

So close your eyes, and breathe deeply. Let the rhythm of your breath calm and refresh you. Let the slow movement of energy in and out of your body bring you to a state of calm, relaxed waiting.

Visualize a soft light building in your heart. As it builds, it takes the shape of a flower—a shining lotus blossom, perhaps, or a white rose with velvet-soft petals. This is your heart—the Divine core of your being, the radiant source of your love. Now visualize the blossom slowly opening, reaching out to you and all that is around you. It glows gently, lit from within.

Say softly to yourself or in your mind:

Blessed Mother, Radiant Father
I open my heart to Your love and Your wisdom.
Help me to see You, hear Your voice, take Your hands.
Help me to find You in myself
Help me to find You all around me.
Blessed be.

As long as the blossom is open, your heart can receive all the blessings of the Lord and Lady. If you close off your heart, concealing its light, They cannot enter and your love cannot be shared. Practice opening your heart, and blessings will follow.

As you perform the Opening Your Heart exercise, preferably over a period of several weeks, pay careful attention to any feelings or perceptions you have immediately afterward. Then at the end of each day, write down in your journal or Book of Shadows everything that you can remember that seemed to have something to do with the exercise: sudden flashes of insight, precognitive experiences, odd coincidences, et cetera. The Lord and Lady very rarely speak to us as a thundering voice from the mountaintop. As I've said, They flow with the natural way of the Earth, so They will most likely speak to you through nature itself.

If you are familiar with the chakra system, try the exercise from a different perspective: visualize each of your chakras opening as a different-colored flower, and ask that they be awakened to Divine mystery. You can also combine this with the attunement in the "Book of Moonlight," which is chakra based, to deepen the experience. The above exercise is short, simple, and easy to perform anywhere in a few minutes so it will be less difficult to add to your daily practice.

This exercise is an important one because, above and beyond any metaphysical changes it may bring, it will at the very least make you more mindful of the Divine in your daily life. In some Buddhist communities, there is a special bell that is rung at certain times during the day. Whenever people hear the bell, they stop, breathe, and become mindful of the present moment. The blossom exercise aims for the same general goal: making you more mindful of the Divine all around you. If you like, you can practice something similar to the Buddhist method by choosing a sound you hear periodically throughout the day such as a telephone, church bells, a doorbell, and so on. When you hear your chosen sound, pause wherever you are, take a deep breath, and visualize the blossom in your heart open fully to Divine love. Such a seemingly simple action can have far-reaching effects on the way you look at your life.

The God and Goddess, the holy interplay between Them, and Their love for all creation are the whole reason for Wicca. They are the ground of our being, the soul of our souls, and the music of the dancing celestial spheres. Seek Them within, and you will find Them everywhere.

THREE THINGS TO THINK ON

1. Do you disagree with the way I have described the God and Goddess? Why? What is different about your own view? How have you heard other people—not just Wiccans—describe Deity?

2. Think back to a time when you truly felt Divine presence, even if it was only for the blink of an eye. What were you doing? Where were you? What about the experience makes it stick out in your mind as sacred? Has it happened since then? If so, what similarities exist among all your experiences?

3. If you aren't sure or haven't ever felt the Lord and Lady near you that you can remember, try the Opening Your Heart exercise for a few weeks and then go back to #2 above. Dur-

ing these weeks, keep your eyes and mind open. Things you may have taken for granted before could assume new importance when you look at them differently.

three

⌐ Living the Path ⌐

THER⌐   ⌐STIVAL.

Yc   the guy in the loincloth, wearing the
thre   's a Third Degree, supposedly, and by
som   a coven made up entirely of nubile
you   of whom make it through their year
an   vithout participating in the Great Rite
(n   wink). He's drunk as a lord most of the
w   ds his time at the bonfire humping
v   rack-addled schnauzer.

               1e's a Wiccan—at least, when no one's
               ks at a giant bloodthirsty corporation,
               her weekdays putting local entrepreneurs
               n weekends she jets around in a gas-guz-
               y vehicle, flicking cigarette butts out the
               she doesn't have the most ethical job in the
               that's business, right? And her crystal-stud-
               $250, so that's supporting the community—
               buy it at the mall.

What am I getting at? In my mind, after the gods-as-magical-tools trend in pop Wicca, the most disturbing thing I've seen is what is commonly known as "Festival Paganism." This is where a person dons her robe and dances the night away over Beltane, and then goes right back to acting as if she had no spiritual life at all the rest of the month. Wicca is not something you do, it's something you *are*—minute to minute. If you learn anything at all from my ranting and raving, learn that.

By now, hopefully, you've given some thought to your relationship with Deity and how you want to deepen and expand it. Before we get into rituals or anything else, however, we must consider how that relationship translates into our daily lives on a less active level. The nature of our view of the universe says a lot about how we should conduct ourselves.

There is more to a personal practice than simply going through the motions. In monastic life, the rule that guides the community covers the entire way of life for its followers, including the standards of behavior and attitude that a monk or nun should strive for day to day. Our own practice, while not founded on a Bible or the ideal set by long-dead saints, should greatly affect the way we act *between* rituals.

As a Wiccan, what sort of picture do you want to present to the world? Whether we realize it or not, every person who finds out about our religious proclivities considers us a portrait of those proclivities. The minute you say, "I am Wiccan," those who hear you begin to build an image in their minds of what that means based on you. Even those of us who are not politically active or working toward our social equality become spokespeople for our religion. If someone sees you breaking promises, treating others with disrespect, or taking candy from babies, the esteem of our religion drops a notch in the public eye. It may not seem fair, but consider how often we do the same thing. There may only be one Baptist holding up a "Jesus hates fags" sign, but he's the one we tend to remember when we talk about "those people."

Think about the term *priestess* or *priest*. What sort of role would a priest have in a community back in the much-debated "good old pre-Christian days?" Or even now? Anyone claiming the title of "priest" would assume a certain responsibility toward his community, whether as a religious leader or simply as a role model for others. The title was never taken lightly.

In Wicca we consider ourselves priestesses of the gods, needing no intermediary between ourselves and the Divine. We have a nested set of circles of responsibility when we step into the role of priestess, as we represent our gods to the larger community. The innermost circle is our responsibility to ourselves to be beings of integrity and compassion. The next circle is our responsibility to our tribe or family, whether by blood or choice; those people close to us whose lives are tightly bound up in our own. Further out is our responsibility to the Pagan community, which can be fulfilled either through service or simply through living ethically. The largest circle is the world, where our actions and their consequences affect people we may never even meet.

Fulfilling our responsibility as sacred beings isn't as difficult as you may think. We need not be Mother Teresa to be a healing force in the world. We have to start with the innermost circle: the individual. There's no way to change the world that isn't one person at a time. People often overlook the self. On the outside we "do unto others," but on the inside there's a patchwork quilt of self-abnegation, societal stereotypes, the opinions of others, and every mean thing anyone has ever said to us eating away at our spirits while we smile at the world.

Far more important than the way others see us is how we see ourselves. The gods do not judge us, but we manage to do so quite well on our own, heaping self-loathing on ourselves that we would never direct toward others. Sometimes we are kinder to our enemies. We are taught from an early age, and by example, to be casually cruel to ourselves: "I'm so fat," "I'm such an idiot," "I must be the ugliest person on Earth." When you find yourself cursing the mirror, stop and think: would you walk up to a total stranger and say, "My god, man, who hit you with the ugly stick?" If you would, put this book down and seek help.

If not, ask yourself why a complete stranger deserves compassion and you don't. You are the God and Goddess as much as any other person. Would you tell your Goddess She's got thunder thighs? If you would, duck.

When it comes to living our path, most of us want rules. Anyone with any sort of ethics has personal standards of behavior. In our spiritual practice, these standards are codified into our own ethical system and become our own "rule," much like the one that guides a monastic community. As Wicca isn't a centuries-old unbroken tradition like many of us would like to think, we are faced with the task of creating our own way of life. You can start with a few basic questions.

How, as a Wiccan and a human being, do you want to treat people? Or yourself?

It has been said that the true measure of a person is how he or she behaves when no one is looking. When it's just ourselves and the gods, there can be no excuses. We Wiccans have a tremendous amount of freedom in our decisions, but that freedom is a two-edged sword. True freedom implies responsibility. We have no devil, no outside source to blame our shortcomings on, and can only look to ourselves for the source of our problems.

Even if we didn't cause a negative situation, we have a choice in how we react to it and what subsequent choices we make to navigate through it. That means that the ever-popular "perpetual victim" syndrome of Western thought—where you cannot be held responsible for your actions because your parents or society or the government or your sixth-grade math teacher hurt your feelings—simply doesn't wash.

Bad things happen. Anyone living on this lovely blue-green planet knows that. The result of our free will is that eventually someone will get in someone else's way, and that someone will either move aside or get shoved. We suffer for things we didn't do, and we get hurt for stupid reasons—it's a fact of life. The important thing isn't so much that shit happens, the important thing is what we do with the shit afterward. We can choose to remain victims, to act out of vengeance or to curl up in a ball and hide, or we can choose to stand up and grow. No one can decide how tragedy will affect us but *us*. Sing or whine, it's our decision. Rather than judging ourselves for our negative emotions or letting suffering determine who we are, we can try to find the lessons beneath our pain. However harsh those lessons may seem, they're always there. Nothing happens without some purpose, even if it's just to teach us not to make the same dumb mistakes over and over. Only when we have learned to put our pain in perspective can we begin the work of turning it into knowledge, of moving from victim to creator.

This kind of knowledge—the wisdom that comes from adversity—doesn't come overnight. Some of our lessons take a lifetime to learn, and there's no one way to learn them. The way to begin is to *choose*. Choose what emotions and behaviors to cultivate in your life—the ones that lead to joy. Choose which to learn from and then release.

Ethics is a minefield in popular discussion. For every law you can come up with, there's at least a dozen exceptions. Even the Wiccan Rede has come under fire as being too simplistic to be of any practical use in society. The Law of Three gets a lot of flak too, although it seems very popular in television portrayals of witches: do something naughty and you'll get it right back. Isn't that handy?

Real life, of course, doesn't always work quite so neatly. The bad guy gets away; the nice girl walks out in front of a crosstown bus on her way to feed the homeless. What happened there? If everything you do comes back threefold, why aren't teachers covered in diamonds and child molesters covered in blood?

The Wiccan Rede is an ethical standard: here's the advice, interpret and follow. The Law of Three, on the other hand, is usually treated as a throwback to our old religious training of "be a good girl or the bogeyman will eat you." We have as a community latched onto this concept because it is a familiar, comfortable model of punishment/reward that we are used to from our Christianity-based society.

We know that on a practical level, quantifying karma does not work. While that sort of scare tactic may be useful with toddlers and pesky adolescents, when you learn to think for yourself, a strict punishment-and-reward system of ethics falls short of reality. When the idiot in the truck cuts you off on the highway, you don't shoot him in the head. It's not because three people will then appear and shoot you, but because you listened to your mother: hurting people is *wrong*.

Ach! you say. A *moral pronouncement! Who are you to tell me what's right and wrong? It's all subjective anyway! What about self-defense? What about righteous retribution?*

Well, fine—shades of gray and all that. Like I said, there's an exception to every rule. The point I'm making, or trying to make, is that if you are of the mindset that everything on Earth is part of the Goddess and God, and that all things are connected, you won't be the sort of person who will need the Law of Three to tell you how to behave. You will see the world as sacred and all beings as sacred and will try to treat them as such. You will understand that for every action there are consequences, and that we make our choices to the best of our ability with the knowledge we have at the time.

We make mistakes; we hurt people by accident, or through carelessness. The goal is not perfection; if we were perfect, we wouldn't be here in the first place. The goal is in the Rede itself: *An' it harm none, do what you will.* We aren't always aware of all of the possible consequences of our actions. We have to make the best decisions we can based on our knowledge and be ready to deal with the fallout.

Some people take the idea of "harm none" as an indication that they shouldn't do anything, because no matter what choice you make, someone will end up getting the short end of the stick. If every breath we take already kills off a million microbes, doesn't that negate the "harm none" end of the Rede for all practical purposes?

What they forget, in my mind, is that the Rede isn't meant to be interpreted literally. As many people have pointed out, the word *rede* itself means "counsel" or "advice," not "law." That's why as an ethical precept it is more realistic than the Law of Three, which sets itself up as an absolute. The eight-word statement of the Rede itself is a *balance*. Balance the harm you do just by living with the good you can do. That, I feel, is an underlying reason why Wiccans are so often called to be healers of one kind or another. We instinctively understand that our beneficial presence in the world helps tip the cosmic scale back from destruction—which the human race is all too fond of—to creation. It is possible, however difficult, to respond to evil with good, to shift the balance back.

Imagine, for a moment, the "perfect" Wiccan. Picture him in your mind. What does he offer to the community? How does he manifest the God and Goddess at work, at the grocery store, with a troubled lover? What does he say to himself when he looks in the mirror? How does he handle adversity?

In my mind I see a woman who is thoughtful, quiet, with a sparkle of mirth in her eyes. When other Pagans need help, she's the one they call. Her inner strength and wisdom speak through her innate respect for all people. Her home is a warm place where her students feel safe, and the door is always open. She tends an herb and vegetable garden in her back yard, where everything is green and a riot of flowers. Small children and animals love her on sight. She volunteers at the local shelter, goes camping, reads voraciously, and is known for her ability to create life-altering rituals. If you could choose one word for this Wiccan it would be *grace*.

What do you see? A powerful priestess at the head of a coven, perhaps, helping her group work toward a better world and better selves? A man living out in the wilderness in a cabin he built with his own hands? There is no one correct image, but the one that comes to your mind says a lot about where you want your spiritual practice to take you. Consider that image and write down all the attributes that make that imaginary person who he is.

I call these attributes "graces." They aren't moral laws, but personal ethical goals. They are the signposts on our path to Deity, and when taken with the Wiccan Rede, can form a strong foundation for our practice. As I said before, people crave rules to tell them how to behave. Our intuitive natures want to go with the flow, to live in tune with nature without giving things so many names. Our logical natures need lines drawn in the sand—definite "yeses" and "nos." Graces, which are guidelines, but not laws, are a sort of compromise: they can grow and change as we do, and are not set in stone, but give us something to light the way between where we are now and where we want to be.

Below are a few graces that I personally try to observe, along with what they mean to my own path.

Wiccan Graces

LOVE

Love should be the cornerstone of any spiritual practice—indeed, it should be the cornerstone of everything. At the risk of sounding a bit too hippie-trippy, in the end, love is all that matters—the love you give, and the love you receive. When you learn to love with a whole heart, without question or limit, you will walk in the footsteps of Deity.

This isn't the traditional Western concept of love, either—a concept that bears the stigmas of rejection, possession, and jealousy. We often confuse love with the addiction that pop songs and movies portray: an endless emotional roller coaster using phrases such as "I need you" or "I'll die without you." Real love—the kind that prophets and mystics have written about and lived for for centuries untold—is unconditional. Love is not interested in taking, but only in giving. The love of the Goddess is poured freely out upon the Earth—even on the evildoers and the biting flies. The goal, then, is to strive to look at the world from a place of love, and to act accordingly.

We all have this love within us, but for most people, it's buried beneath a haystack of conflicting desires, attachments, and pain. Cultivating love for all creatures—for all creation—is a lifelong quest. All of the other graces are facets of love or ways to help us find it in ourselves and others.

COMPASSION

Compassion flows naturally from love into *service*. It's a hard grace to hold; if you see with compassion for all beings, you see the hate and misery that weigh so many of us down, and you see the seeming impossibility of doing anything about it. Wiccans are a healing people at heart, and I've seen a great many of us shut down and box ourselves in from the world because "what can one person do?"

The truth is, not a lot—at least not all at once—but the point is not to right all the wrongs of the world by yourself. The point is that each little act of compassion adds a little healing to a planet whose occupants have spun dangerously out of control. So what if you can only feed one homeless person at a time, or clean up one park? That's one more person with a full belly and one more tree without beer cans around its roots. Wiccans do these things, not simply because of karma or liberal guilt, but because helping and healing are good things to do. Even one candle sheds light.

Learning compassion eventually means unlearning hatred. As you come to see all people with empathy simply because they are human like you and they deserve it, you will find yourself unable to hate. After all, how far is it to travel from our own life to another's? How would you have acted given the same circumstances and surroundings as, say, a fundamentalist who genuinely believes that your religion equals damnation?

This doesn't mean that we can excuse the hateful actions of others. Everyone is ultimately responsible for their own choices, and there are some people—serial killers, rapists, and so on—whose lives we cannot imagine. Compassion, however, means understanding that whatever would drive a person to commit heinous acts against her fellow creatures must have caused that person incredible misery, confusion, and self-loathing, which anyone can relate to.

Compassion is a gateway to love. When you find yourself sitting in your car, watching the homeless man with the hand-lettered sign that says "Will be president for food," and you feel an upwelling of tenderness for someone who can still joke despite his sunburned face and protruding ribs, you are learning what it is to feel real, spiritual love.

Compassion is rarely comfortable. In fact, it can hurt like hell until you learn how best to use it and put it into perspective. Not everyone is suited to work in a shelter, a hospice, or on the streets, but everyone has something to give the world. Part of finding our life's work is figuring out what we can do with the gifts we have, and how our gifts can be gifts for others. Something as small and seemingly insignificant as a get-well card for a coworker is a healing touch on the Earth.

FORGIVENESS

Despite what some cultures would like to believe, there is nothing holy about a grudge. Resentment is such a close cousin of hatred that it can be even more dangerous. It is insidious, because we consider our feelings justified and tend to nurse them, holding them close to our hearts without realizing that they are poisoning us. Anger can be a beneficial thing, because it can force us to take action to stop an intolerable situation, but only if we move through our anger and use it—not let it use us. Acting out of anger is acting thoughtlessly, and very few people can honestly say that doing so left them without any regrets. When we are injured, we must forgive, or eventually our resentment will eat us alive. The longer we hold past actions against someone, the longer we are the victims of their actions.

That being said, I don't think that forgiving others is the biggest obstacle. I think a larger problem is forgiving ourselves. Wicca is supposed to be a religion without guilt; we have no concept of sin, no hell to roast in. We do our best. Even when we do, however, we judge ourselves so harshly that our best might as well have been nothing at all, at least in our own eyes. I know people who keep a running catalog of all the wrongs they've done—all the accidental insults, every little petty thought they've ever harbored—and it dogs their every step.

That is one area where Christianity seems to have us beat. Their God is (occasionally) a forgiving God, and if, for instance, a Catholic confesses his sins and performs the proper penance, all is forgiven. Unfortunately, in the Wiccan view of the universe in which our actions resonate through all the worlds and we change the world with every breath, it isn't so easy to shake off our wrongdoings. Our god didn't have his own son killed to take care of our sins; we are responsible for ourselves, and our shoulders are often bent beneath the weight of self-imposed guilt.

What to do? Well, the most effective way to reach self-forgiveness is through the second grace: compassion. Look at yourself in the mirror and remember that you are a child of the gods—no less perfect or beautiful than the trees or the sky—and that if you made a mistake in the past, you can't go back and change it. You can, however, choose what happens tomorrow. Say to yourself, "I am a priestess of the Goddess, and I choose to do better." Have compassion for yourself and try again. It is hard in this society to learn self-love, but it can be done one choice at a time.

Humor

Yes, the gods are laughing at you. Who wouldn't? I happen to think the Lord and Lady find me hilarious. One thing not to forget is this: take your religion seriously, but don't take yourself too seriously. I've heard too many stories about rituals gone awry, altars and billowing sleeves catching fire, invocations rife with Freudian slips, and bees flying down the front of priestesses' robes to think ritual is supposed to be a solemn and somber affair. The minute you begin to take yourself too seriously, the Lord and Lady will send you a gentle (and generally embarrassing) reminder that the universe, by and large, is a joyous place to be.

Case in point: toward the beginning of my Pagan career, a friend and I decided to put on a full moon ritual to show a Christian friend of ours what it was like to be one of "those people." We went all out: robes, special candles, a huge altar, incense thicker than the air in Los Angeles. Our friend was appropriately awed, and I went to the center of the Circle to invoke the Lord and Lady, athame in hand.

I raised the athame dramatically, saying something pretentious, and *smack!* slammed the blade into the overhead light. Glass rained down all around my head, catching the candlelight and throwing sparkles all about the room. I stood there beet-red, wondering what to do next.

Our friend, sitting in the Eastern quarter, gasped with huge eyes, "Wow . . . you guys are *good*."

GRATITUDE

Westerners are a bit unclear on the idea of gratitude. We think we should only be thankful when we've asked for something—begged for it even—and our prayers are answered in the form we wanted them to be. We forget to be thankful for the simple miracle of just being. What blessing is greater than to live on this beautiful planet amidst the trees and grass and sea and sky, with so much possibility all around us? The Earth, and our lives, renew themselves every day. In this way, the Christians have the right idea: count your blessings! Include thankfulness in your devotions to the Lord and Lady, and if nothing else, your sense of wonder about the world and the mystery of life will widen. As an example, in the "Book of Moonlight" in part two I have included a simple ritual of gratitude. Try it, or use it to create your own.

INTEGRITY

This is a tough one in today's society, where honesty has very little value except on children's television. I don't mean telling the absolute brutal truth no matter what the situation, thereby assuring you will hurt someone and make a lot of enemies. I'm talking about integrity; walking the talk.

There is an old saying that "a witch's word is law." There are many ways to interpret that, but I choose to see it as a statement of integrity: when I say I will do something, I do it. Promises were *not* made to be broken. Back in the days of yore it is said that breaking your word was tantamount to mowing down your tribe with flaming arrows.

Vowing never to break your word means you take care when you give it—you don't fling meaningless promises around. Americans in particular are all about big talk and very little about action. As hard as it is to define truth, as beings of integrity we must strive to be as truthful as we can.

There is a difference between carefully choosing your words so as not to reveal everything all at once and telling a lie. Lies erode our self-worth, our respect for ourselves and others, and do the world no good in the long run—but then, neither does blurting out exactly what you think about every little thing. There is a time for truth—for words—and there is a time for silence. We could do with a bit more silence *and* a bit more truth.

How can you have both? By making your words fewer and the truth behind them greater. By picking your battles and deciding when it's appropriate to speak up and when it's more appropriate to act (or not to act). When presented with a picture of a coworker's baby, instead of saying, "My god, who shagged an iguana?" you might try, "Oh, she has her father's eyes!"

WISDOM

One criticism of Wiccans is that we are, shall we say, a little unconcerned about our mythology. No, that's putting it mildly—we're largely ignorant. By and large, people are willing to take what is said in a book, or maybe two, and consider it gospel, just as we were taught in the patriarchy most of us ran from. It makes us look like total idiots in the religious community.

What does this have to do with Wiccan ethics?

Well, looking back at the idea of integrity, how can we practice what we preach if we don't even know what we're preaching? Knowledge—real knowledge gained through research and paying attention—is one of the most powerful tools humans have against bigotry and hatred. It's much easier to discuss (not argue, which never gets anyone anywhere) theology with someone when you've done your homework. It's more effective to do a ritual in Latin when you know what the words actually mean. It's easy to banter about trivia we've memorized, like in high school, but true wisdom is both the knowing of a thing and the understanding of it. All the correspondence tables in the world can't help you cast a spell if you have to read the entire thing from a script.

There is a difference, I might add, between knowledge and wisdom, but both are important on a spiritual path. Knowledge is the information we gain from outside sources, whether they're books or other people. Personal wisdom is our own hard-won combination of knowledge plus experience, plus the understanding gleaned from both. Spiritual wisdom is the underlying truth in things; the lessons we can learn from nature and the world, lessons we have to seek out or stumble into.

At the same time that we hold our own knowledge cheaply, we discriminate against the wisdom of our elders. By elders I mean those whose wisdom comes from real day-to-day experience and interaction with the spiritual ideas we want to embrace. These elders may not necessarily be older in years, but their learning and maturity speaks of great age. True wisdom can come from anywhere: a child, a rose, your cat, the homeless man on the corner. Listen and learn.

For instance, I was waiting in line at the grocery store one Sunday, and to make conversation while he scanned my purchases, the clerk asked, "So, did you go to church today?"

"No," I replied, smiling.

"Me neither," he said with a grin. "Do you usually go?"

I decided to go with the truth, even though I didn't particularly feel like being the Wiccan poster child that morning. "No, I don't—I'm not a Christian. I'm Wiccan."

His grin broadened, and he nodded. "Oh, yeah, so's my cousin. I guess that means you're at church pretty much all the time, eh?"

Talk about a cosmic two-by-four! A random stranger imparted the most profound wisdom I heard that entire week. I wonder what he'll say next time.

Joy

As your capacity for love grows, so will your capacity for joy. This doesn't mean a giddy whirlwind of happiness, either. As with love, we often mistake real joy for something similar but ultimately less fulfilling. Joy exists in two forms. First, there are the moments when you pause, look around, and say to yourself, "This is really good." Those are the times when nothing needs perfecting, nothing is amiss. However fleeting they may be, these moments make all our striving worthwhile. Second, joy exists as an undercurrent of a life lived according to our graces. When your words, actions, and heart are all in line, joy will take root and wind itself around your life like a moonflower vine. You won't constantly be aware of it, but people who know you will see it in your eyes, hear it in your voice, and respond to its warmth.

Growth

As we can see easily in nature, all things must grow and change or wither away and die. The opposite of growth is stagnation. We allow our lives to stagnate at times, clinging to outmoded ideas and routines and following habits that do not serve our spiritual progress. Advertising would have us believe that any problem, any personal fault, can be remedied with the right product or the right book—all in less than a week. We chase after these quick-fix solutions, only to find ourselves right back in a rut when the "solutions" prove empty.

We have forgotten in our haste that growth and change are a *process*. How do the roots of a tree break through boulders? One millimeter at a time, day by day, taking it slowly. Going from seed to great oak is a massive undertaking, and it happens in a gentle unfolding over years and years. Again, in our human arrogance, we have assumed that we are somehow different from the other inhabitants of our blue-green world.

Silly humans, say the trees. *Just shut up and grow.*

All of these ethical and behavioral ideas may seem like a lot to accomplish, but the most effective way to dance with the graces is to be mindful of them. Become aware of the things you say, the actions you take, and how they correspond to your belief system. I've heard people say that the difference between good and evil is that good cares. It's not so much the actions in and of themselves as the intent behind them and our awareness of their effect on the rest of the world.

Mindfulness is the key. Most of the unethical things we do stem from negligence that makes us say things we don't mean and do things when we know better.

Finally, and very importantly, don't forget to apply the graces to how you treat yourself. Your life is holy. Your heart and mind and body are expressions of Divine love, and if you don't treat them as such, who will?

THREE THINGS TO THINK ON

1. Consider each of the graces in turn, and choose one that you feel you are lacking in your life. What one thing, no matter how small, could you do each day to bring more of that grace into your path? Are there any personal graces you would add to the list—ideals you feel are vital to your spiritual life? Form a set of your own graces and write them down, adding them to the concepts you formed from the previous chapter. Also, how do you already manifest the graces day by day? Where are your strengths? What do you have to be proud of in the way you treat the others around you (not just people; your pets, your houseplants, your planet)?

2. When you have compiled a list of your graces, write them out along with your other beliefs in a sort of pledge, or ethical code. Begin your statements with "I believe," "I pledge," "I will strive for," or some other phrase that suits you, and adopt these statements as your credo. Keep them in your Book of Shadows or other magical/spiritual record where you can review them often. Post them on the wall near your altar. Carry them on a card in your wallet—anything that will keep you mindful of them.

3. In the "Book of Moonlight" in part two you will find a ritual of self-blessing. This or any similar rite you can create will help you remember to treat yourself with love and compassion, especially if performed regularly.

four

⌐ The Temple Hearth ¬

OUT IN THE WORLD, WE may be misunderstood. Our beliefs may be twisted into bad science fiction or pseudo-demonic tripe. Our government officials may claim we don't practice a "real" religion. The ethics and spirituality we work so hard to nourish may be treated like New Age nonsense—condemned, laughed at, belittled. Just spending a day at the office can be enough to make us want to go live in a cave in the Appalachians and raise goats.

Then, there's home.

A Wiccan's home isn't merely his castle, it's his sanctuary, where the conflicting demands and opinions of society fade away into mist. There, surrounded by the belongings and ideas we choose, we can shed our workaday personas and just be who we are. Outside our doors, the Goddess is relegated to grade-school mythology and pigeonholed as "feminist" rhetoric. Inside, Her worship continues undaunted, held fast in hundreds of living rooms and bedrooms across the country.

The original purpose of an indoor dwelling was, of course, protection. It still is, although the elements and wandering saber-toothed tigers aren't as much of a danger as they used to be. Nowadays our main concern is keeping the world that humans have created from grinding our spirits under its giant, polluted, politicized, commercialized heel. We spend all day battling the stereotypes of an uncaring society, trying by example to undo centuries of bad press. When we come home, we want to lay down our arms and armor.

It doesn't matter whether you live in a palatial five-bedroom house or a four-hundred-square-foot efficiency apartment; the space you occupy is your own, and can reflect your deepest values and beliefs. Even if you share a room with two med students and their pet boa constrictor, some measure of space—a shelf, a wall, your desk—can be devoted to your devotion. If you are fortunate enough to live alone or with like-minded people, the whole house is your temple, waiting to be adorned in honor of your gods and your heart.

Despite the traditional Wiccan concept of sacred space, which calls for a formally cast Circle to be erected and taken down for every ritual, most Wiccans end up having a sort of permanent Circle set up in their homes. Often this isn't even intentional; years of magic and reverence will consecrate a space just as thoroughly as a two-hour house blessing rite.

If you've ever stood inside one of the few remaining ancient sacred places—a stone circle, a ring of oak trees, an old church—you know the feeling, the hush that comes over you when you step onto hallowed ground. There's a subtle difference in the air, perhaps not as obvious as within a cast

Circle, but peaceful and restive all the same. With care, attention, and energy, we can recreate this feeling in a gentler fashion in our own homes.

How do you achieve this? Everyone's home is different, and so are our feelings about what makes a space sacred. There are, however, a few steps you can take to get started transforming a seemingly mundane apartment or house into a temple of Divine mystery.

It starts with a sense of priority. Stand in the middle of your bedroom or living room and look around. This is your space. What is it missing? What's already there? What about your home feeds your spirit and adds to your daily practice? What could you add?

Often the main thing standing between our homes and their true potential is dirt—both physical and psychic. Even if nothing particularly nasty has gone on in your life recently, the air in your home may still seem a little heavy. Think of your emotional baggage as dust; when you come in the door, you track it in, and it gets ground into the carpet or settles in the corners. You may start to get cabin fever, especially after you've spent large amounts of time shut in the house, say during the winter. It's not just a need to be up and moving around—living things give off energy, and if the atmosphere isn't flowing properly, that energy has nowhere to go, and it will stagnate. The solution is the time-honored tradition of house cleansing.

Cleansing the Home

Few people really enjoy housework, but I've noticed that highly spiritual people in general have an easier time with it. In monastic communities, work is treated as a form of prayer, a holy sharing of skills that benefits the community as well as the soul. Before even lighting a stick of incense, clean your home from top to bottom, keeping in mind the higher purpose of the task. You are making way for the Divine to inhabit the space you inhabit, and keeping your temple a fitting site for the miraculous. Some kitchen witches even consecrate their mop water and add essential oils such as lemon and orange, which not only act as disinfectants, but are known for their spiritually cleansing properties.

You may also want to limit your household cleaning products to those that are environmentally friendly. Most commercially available cleansers are highly toxic, or at least irritating, and are neither good for the body nor the planet. Bleach may kill germs, but it can also kill you and your pets. Even ingested in the tiny amounts in cleaning residue, over time bleach can make you sick if it isn't rinsed with enough water. There are a variety of products on the market nowadays that are less scary. In a pinch, baking soda and white vinegar can clean just about anything. Annie Berthold-Bond's wonderful book *Clean and Green* is an invaluable resource for nontoxic housecleaning.

Only you can decide how clean is clean enough. Some people are natural clutter-bugs, myself included. Every available surface in my home is covered in candles, natural objects, and figures of animals, goddesses, and a wide variety of other things. Others might have a coronary at the thought of so many dust-catchers and lean toward the simple. To you, the house may not be clean until the windows are sparkling. My windows haven't seen a rag since I moved in, but the kitchen has to be spotless or I can't sleep. Cleanliness is next to godliness, they say, and godliness is rather subjective.

After all the physical gunk is gone from the area, begin a spiritual cleansing of the space. Smudge the area with a favorite incense or one that is considered appropriate for the job—sage and lavender are two of many herbs recommended for purification. Sprinkle blessed salt water, perhaps, moving around the perimeter of your home. Another alternative is to create an herbal blessing powder for purification, protection, or any other sacred purpose you would like to imbue your home with. Sprinkle it around the house, and then vacuum up the excess. If your powder is mixed with a little baking soda, this will freshen the carpets as well as charge the room.

Don't forget closets, bathrooms, laundry rooms, and the garage. You may wish to chant as you walk, either something melodic that moves you or a simple sentence or two such as, "I *cleanse this home by Earth and Water, that only beauty and truth may enter.*" Alternately, crank up some lively music and dance around the house as you cleanse. Whatever moves your spirit will move energy.

Once your home has been cleansed, pause for a while and consider. Just as you created a mental image of the "perfect" Wiccan in the previous chapter, now imagine the "perfect" home for that person. Don't limit yourself to where you live now—let yourself dream. Let your mind build a cottage deep in the woods, or a rambling two-story house on the edge of town surrounded by overgrown herb and vegetable gardens. Perhaps the ultimate place to you is an urban penthouse with a view of the city spread out all around, or a farm way out in the country.

Mentally explore this special place, taking note of the things that make it the sacred home it is. Do you see particular decorations, furniture, or colors? What sort of things can you see yourself doing there?

These fantasies can give you surprising insight into what you really want your home to be. You may tell yourself that, as a Wiccan, you're supposed to want a country house with climbing vines and a dozen cats, when in reality the perfect witch's cottage to you would be an upscale townhouse decorated in tribal prints and artifacts. Don't let what you're "supposed" to be cloud who you really want to be, or who you really are. There is no one exact way to be Wiccan.

Perhaps instead of a specific home, you dream of a place out in the wild somewhere that to you would be the ideal sacred space. What if your home were in a grove of oak and aspen, or inside a crystal cave? These images, too, can contribute to your efforts. They give you a feeling to aim for, an atmosphere.

Now look around at the place where you live and appraise it in terms of the image in your mind. Where could you change things to create a bridge between the ideal and the real? You'd be surprised what a difference simply moving the furniture around can make. Dozens of books on feng shui, the Chinese art of placement, are devoted to just that concept.

Find a place, however small or out-of-the-way, where you could build an altar. All the wonderful tools and toys of the Craft you have collected will do you a lot more good out where you can see and use them regularly than they will packed away under the bed between rituals.

If you are a traditionalist and the idea of a permanent altar doesn't sit well, try a shrine instead—a place for sacred contemplation and prayer, but not necessarily ritual work or magic. You can have little shrines all over the house dedicated to different facets of the Divine and of your life, and then erect an altar for rituals independent of your shrines. An important consideration is that a permanent altar can collect dust, so if you want to have one, you must commit yourself to its care. Keep it clean, and work with it daily.

A shrine, at the very least, is almost necessary for a daily religious practice. You will find you need some place to go— a place that serves as a focus, a place of pause. It's perfectly fine to pray sitting on your couch, but sitting in front of a special spot adorned with items that are sacred to you and lighting a candle set aside for that purpose will prove far more beneficial to your practice, especially in the beginning while you are establishing a routine.

A personal altar isn't just a place to practice, it's a declaration; a way of saying that you are your own clergy. You no longer have to go outside, to another building built and decorated by someone else, to give honor to the Divine. Sacred objects and tools aren't just the hands of the privileged few, while you stay out among the masses listening to a sermon someone else wrote. Your spirituality is your own, centered around your private life, your private worship. A personal altar is a physical affirmation of our inner selves. No one has the right to dictate its size, shape, or intent but its priest—you.

There are all sorts of places to build shrines and altars, and a lack of space or an abundance of nosy pets shouldn't deter you. I have seen lovely sacred spaces on bookshelves, computer desks, the top of a refrigerator, in a closet, on a bedside table, and even in a medicine cabinet. If the only place you ever get a moment alone in your busy family life is in the bathroom, so be it. Hang a little shelf in the shower up above where the water reaches, and look for waterproof objects to place there. Wall shelves are especially nice for people with cats or toddlers, since they can be hung above arm's or paw's reach. Look at your home with new eyes, seeking out the little nooks and corners that you can dedicate to your spiritual practice. Let your imagination and intuition guide you.

Altar diagrams abound in Wiccan books, but in reality, no two altars that I have seen are alike. It's not so important where you place your tools on your altar as it is that you know why you put them there. Do you want to divide your altar into elemental quarters, or have one side dedicated to the Goddess and the other to the God? Perhaps such a formal arrangement doesn't feel appropriate, and you want to lay things out by how they look and feel "happiest." You'll know when it's right. Your shrine or altar is highly personal and needs to please you, not someone else's diagram.

Having decided what you want your sacred space to be, the next thing is to dedicate and consecrate it as your home temple. There are a number of already-written rituals for just that, and another is included in the "Book of Moonlight" that you may want to look at, dissect, and adapt for your own needs. The primary purpose of these rituals is to declare your intention to treat your home as a place of worship and magic, then raise energy to empower its walls with its new purpose. Many house blessing rituals also include cleansing, which you have hopefully already done. You can either omit these steps or do them again, since according to grandmothers everywhere, a house can never be too clean.

Magical Tools and Religious Practice

What place do all those nifty tools and trappings have in a spiritual practice when spellcasting is not the most important activity? While it's true that the only tools you need are an open mind and heart and a pair of hands, ritual tools serve an important function on any religious path. Imagine a Catholic mass without incense, candles, robes, or an altar. The words might still be moving to the congregation, but it just wouldn't "feel the same." All of the toys we use add extra dimensions to our practice and anchor our spirituality in the senses.

As I mentioned before, Wicca is a sensual religion, involving the body as much as the mind. Tools help engage all our senses, including the ones we aren't always aware of. They are especially important when conducting rituals indoors, away from the wonderful sensory experiences of the natural world. That is the entire purpose of tools: they help us move past "mundane" reality into a state of awareness where magic can happen.

Most Wicca 101 books give details about magical tools and their symbolism, so I won't. But there are some things you might want to add to your inventory of tools that will enhance your devotional practice.

A Devotional Candle

Any color, any size, any type will do, though I've found that the seven-day glass Catholic votives work beautifully. They're inexpensive, pretty, they last a while, and you can reuse the glass as a vase, incense holder, or a variety of other things. You can also decorate them with decoupage or glass paint. As far as colors go, white is probably your best bet as its symbolism is manifold and its purity will not be distracting as some brighter hues might be. The purpose of this candle is to serve as a sort of signal for your inner self that you are doing something holy. Light it every time you pray, do a ritual, or anything else that is part of your spiritual practice. After a while you will be able to shift at least partway into the mindset of "something sacred's about to happen" just by looking at its flame.

A House Incense

Everyone has a favorite scent. Try different incenses until you find one that bespeaks the feeling you want to promote in your home, and stock up on it. Burn it several times a week to keep the energy in your home flowing. Nag Champa and sandalwood are both very popular—remember to choose something that will please yourself, anyone who dwells with you, and the people you choose to invite in. As much as you may love the smell of burning valerian (yuck!), your significant other may take one whiff and run for the hills. You may want a summer scent and a winter one, or perhaps one for each season, or simply stick to one that feels right year round. Change it, of course, as your own growth dictates. For instance, an ex-lover of mine was incredibly fond of Nag Champa, so while we lived together we burned it constantly. While I loved the scent at the time, after the relationship imploded, I could no longer stand the smell of it and gave away every last stick. It was quite a while before I could burn it again, as the aroma immediately reminded me of dirty dishes and broken promises, but in the meantime I had grown into a nice amber blend that I still use.

Natural Objects

Bring nature indoors as much as possible. As much as we'd prefer to do all our rituals on a grassy plain or deep in the woods, weather, time, and location don't always cooperate. The majority of your practice will be conducted at home, and if you don't have a backyard or a park within a stone's throw, you may have to work hard to schedule time with the Earth. Aim for at least once a week, but in the meantime, gather a few things that help you recall the love of the Goddess and God and the beauty of the world around us. Stones, leaves, seeds, feathers, anything that calls to you that won't involve you being shot for trespassing or injuring the environment are all lovely reminders of our true teachers and can also keep us in touch with the seasons when we aren't able to commune with nature as often as we'd like.

An Offering Pouch

While we're on the subject of rituals outdoors, you may find it appropriate to carry with you a little bag of something to offer the environment whenever you have spent time with it meditating, praying, or simply being. Nature gives so much to us so unselfishly; we should endeavor to give back. Fill your pouch with things the local critters will like but that won't upset the ecosystem. Seeds are fine, but make sure they are toasted or ground up so they won't sprout and invade the local flora. My pouch has sunflower seeds, pumpkin seeds, cornmeal, lavender, and local wildflower seeds. A hint: be sure your pouch or bag can zip. A plain drawstring will almost certainly come open and spill its contents all over your purse or backpack, which can cause problems with marauding squirrels.

Your Book of Shadows

If you don't already have one, now is the time to start a Book of Shadows. A Book of Shadows doesn't have to be a dry recipe book of spells and rituals—it can be a prayer book, a place to seek inspiration, a comforting old friend. Fill your Book with quotations, prayers, poetry, invocations, artwork, and all the details of your personal practice, and let it occupy a special place on your altar. Your Book is the atlas of your spirit, its maps drawn by your own hand to guide you down your path.

Altar Dressing

My favorite approach to altar decoration, and the one most in keeping with the ever-changing natural world, is to re-dress your altar with the seasons. Change the natural objects that adorn it as the world outside changes. Change the colors of your altar cloths and candles. Add your own sacred objects, such as photographs, quotations, and symbols of your goals, and let them evolve as your life evolves. Our altars, as I said, are a reflection of our inner lives, so they should never remain static. They should also be dusted from time to time; sneezing fits and open flames do not mix.

My own altar is a sofa table that I finished by hand, and at present it lives in my bedroom. It's the first thing I see upon rising each morning. I loved the color of the wood so much that instead of draping it with a full altar cloth, I bought a variety of woven cotton placemats to serve as a sort of "working cloth." They're inexpensive, pretty, and catch wax drips that might damage the wood beneath. I change the mat each sabbat or if I'm doing a big important ritual that calls for its own color (such as black for banishing).

Aside from the traditional Wiccan tools—athame, pentacle, chalice, salt and water bowls, et cetera—my altar is crowded with all sorts of treasures, each with its own story. It's never the same altar twice; I'm always moving something, adding or taking away. A blue hand-blown glass bird my mother gave me sits beside a tiny laughing Ho-Tei, who stands at the feet of my most recent acquisition, a soft sculpture Goddess with Her arms outspread in benediction. There are shells, a basket of stones, stalks of wheat and maize, an amethyst cluster, my mortar and pestle, and a strand of rose quartz chips interwoven with sandalwood mala beads. I have leaves from the trees that stand watch over my apartment, and not long ago I found the sun-bleached claws of a hermit crab in the creek a few miles from home, which now resides in a shell with a hunk of rough amber and some cherimoya seeds.

None of these things are strictly necessary for my practice, but they all nurture my spirit. When I come home after a long day fending off the mundane, light my prayer candle and a stick of sandalwood incense, and take a few minutes to sit and breathe in front of my altar, my eyes linger on the many little objects that the God and Goddess have gifted me with to celebrate Their love, and I smile at the way the candlelight makes the bluebird glow and the Buddha dance. Just the act of settling in front of your altar can be enough to shift your consciousness into a sacred frame of mind.

In order for that to happen, however, your altar has to speak to you. Several friends of mine prefer a more Spartan approach—especially, I've noticed, the men. Their altars are a tribute to beauty in simplicity: a few candles, their tools, perhaps a potted plant. Clean lines and understated geometrical shapes have an elegance that harkens back to the Grecian temples. I've been told that too much stuff can be distracting, and I can see how that would be important. Having too many things to look at could keep you from focusing on the connection between yourself and the Divine, particularly if your housekeeping skills are a bit lax. While you should be meditating you're thinking, "I really need to dust in here." I'm just so used to my clutter that it instantly says "altar" to me, and all my knick-knacks give me quiet moments of joy. Both approaches are equally valid, of course, and you'll see both extremes and every shade in between in the wondrous variety of Wiccan altars.

Just as your home needs periodic cleansing and charging, so, too, does your altar. You'll find that taking down your altar and rebuilding it from the ground up is a very inspiring ritual. The care and attention you give to each piece, cleaning it gently before returning it to its home, will keep the spiritual energy of your sacred space flowing freely and joyfully.

Devotional Sacred Space

No discussion of personal sacred space would be complete without the Wiccan Circle.

For most magical acts and rituals, the Circle serves several important functions. First, it is a barrier, keeping out unwanted influences that might distract or otherwise interfere with the goings-on. While most Wiccans don't get too hung up about the astral nasties that might invade a ritual, it has been known to happen on rare occasions. Anytime you make noise between the worlds, something unsavory is bound to hear. Beyond that, though, a Circle can keep out more mundane distractions that are far more likely to be a problem. Very often sounds from the outside world become muffled, and sometimes people have been known to walk right past a ritual without having the faintest idea anything was going on. It's as though the cast Circle creates a sort of cloak between magical and mundane reality. How else could you explain a group of twenty people in black robes chanting and waving wands while the pedestrians of downtown Austin walk past without batting an eye? (Even in a city where the homeless frequently dress in drag, that's stretching credulity a bit.)

Secondly, a Circle functions as a container for the energy you raise during ritual. Without something to put it in, energy is without form or direction and can't really be put to much practical use. The most oft-used analogy is that in order to boil water, you need a pot. This, I believe, is a more important reason for a Circle than a barrier, since psychic disturbance is fairly uncommon and good common sense can minimize most mundane distractions. We pull energy from the Earth, and usually some from ourselves, to create a sort of paddock for our magic to gallop around in, kicking up its heels until we're ready to let it run to its destination.

The third function of a Circle is as sacred space, which is its most basic and necessary spiritual purpose. Wiccans don't have to go to a church to commune with our gods; as They exist everywhere, our "churches" can be everywhere, any time.

There is, however, a problem inherent in the traditional Circle when it comes to rituals of pure celebration or communion with Deity. When we create a Circle, ideally we set up a space that is not a space, temporarily disconnecting a small pocket of the world from its surroundings. When doing magic this is necessary for protection and structure, as we've already mentioned, and it works quite well—too well, sometimes. If you have entered the Circle to commune with the Lord and Lady, being in an area that has been "set aside" from the rest of the world might not be entirely appropriate. I've been in Circles that were so expertly cast that they felt like they were somewhere else entirely, cut off from the whole natural world where even the breezes didn't blow. I can't help but feel that for rituals that are purely worship or for prayer and meditation, severing yourself from nature is defeating the purpose.

Traditionalists will argue with me, but I am in no way advocating that we give up casting Circles. As I said, they serve a vital purpose in magical work. If, on the other hand, you have trekked out into the woods to do a ritual honoring the Forest Lord, you'll find that casting a formal Circle is completely unnecessary with the elements whirling around you and the Divine whispering from behind every tree.

Casting Circles for every ritual seems doubly superfluous if we consider the home a temple and have consecrated it as such. If your home is a permanent Circle—even an informal one—adding another barrier to what's already there is, in most cases, shooting flies with an elephant gun. There will always be times when you want the added protection, or when things in your home are so insane that a wall between your sacred space and your housemates is just what you need, but in the case of most intimate rituals and meditations, doubling up the protective energy around you isn't terribly important.

In the quiet of your ritual space at home, sitting down and lighting your candles may be all the declaration of sacred space you need. The point isn't so much to create sacred space as to recognize that it already exists everywhere and in everything. The sacred space is actually created in your heart rather than in a place—or, less poetically put, the beginning of a ritual signals to your inner self that you are in a place of reverence, and the rational part of your mind steps back to let spirit flow.

Even without the need for a formally cast Circle, we still crave structure in all our rituals. So a compromise must be made between the traditional Circle and just jumping into things. Really all that you have to do to make a typical Circle-casting appropriate for a nonmagical ritual is to leave out the casting itself, where energy is used to erect the Circle's boundary. Certainly we still desire the presence of the elements and Deity no matter what our purpose, but without the need for a barrier to protect us or contain magical energy, we can take a gentler approach.

For example, suppose your daily practice involves half an hour of meditation in the evenings, but you feel oddly disjointed if you just sit down and start meditating without any preparation. To give the meditation time a more spiritual slant, you can declare sacred space, perhaps in the following manner.

Sit before your altar and take a few deep breaths to still your mind. Light your prayer candle and, if you wish, incense—the scent is up to you, though if you're meditating, the smell might distract you.

Silently, or aloud, call to the elements and invite them to join you in your meditation (or devotion, or whatever you're doing). You aren't asking for them to build a Circle around you, but just to be present in and around you and lend whatever sort of hand you may need in the course of your meditation. You could even call to them all in one invocation rather than individually.

Next, of course, call to the God and Goddess. It's always best to speak from the heart, and in informal rituals by yourself you don't have to worry if words escape you and all you can manage is, "Hi, Mom." It's also a good idea just on general principle to have one or two short invocations memorized.

Finally, say out loud why you're there, and what you're up to. It's very important, no matter how unscripted your rites are, to state your purpose. It keeps you focused and helps ensure that you have given plenty of thought to the reason you are doing what you're doing in the first place.

Since you haven't raised any energy for the Circle, you don't have to worry about cutting a doorway if you need to leave, or, for that matter, releasing the Circle when you're done. For continuity, courtesy, and closure, though, I recommend bidding farewell to the Lord and Lady and then to the elements.

The cyclical nature of Wiccan ritual—from casting the Circle to opening it at the end—is a microcosm of the cycles of the universe: the life cycle, the orbits of the planets, the movement of water through the environment, even the evolution of cultures. Therefore, you wouldn't want to leave it unfinished as it would throw the whole symbolism off balance and could negatively affect your ritual. Everyone has been to a ritual where the Circle-casting took an hour and the closing took two minutes. That unfinished feeling where things are left hanging stays with the people involved, and any energy raised to form the Circle to begin with drifts about until it moves elsewhere.

In a ritual without a formal casting, you have still called a certain amount of energy. Anything you do, whether magical or mundane, causes some kind of stir in the universe. It is the considerate and balanced thing to do to give your rites a definite ending so that the ripples in the universal pond can settle and the room can return to "normal."

CASTING THE WEB OF LIFE

On the subject of sacred space, there is one more thing I'd like to talk about before we move on to the next chapter: the concept of reconnection with the natural world. Our society forces us to live at an unnatural pace, working in toxic offices filled with recycled, stale air and no windows. We go from house to car to work to car to house again, often without even noticing the weather—we dress for the climate at work, not outside. We know all about shopping on the Internet, but have no idea where our drinking water comes from. We are disconnected from nature, wounded from the spirit outward, and that wound has caused the largest majority of the problems that plague our world today.

In a society where the Earth is considered sacred, the rainforests would thrive. In a culture where all things are divine, sexism and racism and any other -ism that separates us from each other along superficial boundaries would have no place at all. Our fundamental, self-enforced separation from the natural world is tantamount to ripping a child from its mother's breast and forcing it to live on Diet Coke.

As with anything that needs to change, the only way to repair the damage is one person at a time. We may not be able—or willing—to abandon our modern lives and seek out homes in the country (I for one couldn't live without bookstores), but we can still reforge our connection to the natural world, to our loving Mother and Father who have been waiting patiently for us to remember Them.

Simple exercises like the following can make all the difference in the world.

Find a place in the natural world that calls to you, no matter how small. At the very least, find a tree to sit against. Get comfortable, and close your eyes. Breathe deeply.

When you are relaxed and calm, reach out with your senses. Become aware of the ground beneath you, the tree at your back, the air on your face. Spend a few moments learning the place you are at, listening to the wind in the treetop or the birds or even the traffic noise. Then, begin to extend your awareness, stretching little by little until you are aware of the next few feet, then the next. With each breath out, let your awareness expand from your body. What does it tell you about the world that surrounds you? Can you "feel" specific forms, such as animals, people, buildings? Is it more of a shimmer to your subconscious? How do you perceive the energy of your environment?

Reach out farther, and now visualize your awareness as the thin strands of a shining web. Let the web spin itself outward, taking your mind with it, farther and farther away from your body. See how the web connects you to the grass, the trees, the people passing by, and eventually to everything that lives. You sit at the center, for this one moment, while the web spins ever outward, joining you to all creation one strand at a time. With each choice, each interaction, each event, the web shifts a little, and the future changes; still you remain connected, bound to the land beneath you and the sky above. All of the laughter, all of the pain, all of the life and death and never-ending change of the world flow through you, around you, with you. As you inhale, all beings of the Earth inhale. You are the weaver, you are the woven, you are the web.

Eventually, begin to draw the strands of the web back toward your body, one breath at a time. Although you are still joined with everything—and always will be—your awareness returns to your individual self. Your breath becomes your own again, and you can look out through your own eyes at the world that lives through you.

THREE THINGS TO THINK ON

1. When you cast a Circle, why do you do it? What does the Circle look or feel like to you? Does it function more as a barrier or a container, both, or neither?

2. Look around your home and identify places that you already treat as sacred. Is there a shelf where your family

pictures are kept, or a spot on your dresser where you set a particularly meaningful item? Check the front of the refrigerator for a surprise shrine to your children, pets, or family.

3. We are all altar builders by instinct. If you were to turn that instinct into purposeful action, where could you build an altar? Assume for a moment that you could move all your furniture, even have a whole room to yourself for just that purpose. How would you arrange it? What would you need?

five

Building a Practice

FROM THE TIME WE RISE each morning until the velvet blue-gray of nightfall, we have many chances to deepen our awareness of Divine mystery. Every activity you engage in can become a ritual full of meaning—whether you are a short-order cook or a high-powered executive or anything in between. This applies to getting out of bed, eating, driving, working, cleaning house, cooking, making love, bathing, going back to bed again, and myriad other moments throughout the day.

Wait, you say. Is all of this attention to detail really going to make me a better Wiccan? Won't all these mini-rituals make me late for work and force me to miss out on my social life to stay home and pray? Won't my friends give me weird looks if I say, "Here, hold my purse. Before I use the restroom I must consecrate the toilet with sage smoke and thrice-blessed oils"?

I hope so, no, and I hope so. In religious practice, as in interior decorating, there is a line between the beautiful and the ridiculous. Fortunately, everyone has an instinctive idea of where that line is in his own path. Remember that our goal is a life of sacred purpose, and that the operative word is *life*. If you deny yourself the pleasures of company or a sense of fun, eventually you will resent your daily rituals and give them up altogether. A spiritual practice should blend seamlessly with and enrich the life you wish to lead, not turn you into a hermit.

Besides, nowhere is it written that religion has to be a solitary art to be a meaningful one. Though the majority of Wiccans nowadays practice alone, and the largest part of your personal path will be walked that way, the coven—and, more importantly, the community—still has a very important place in our spiritual lives. The joy of others amplifies our own joy, and aside from nature, other people are our greatest teachers.

I suggest that you start simply. Read through this chapter and select a few ideas you think would work well with your life, or that you are willing to slightly rearrange your life for. For instance, start with prayers at mealtimes, which most people are already familiar with, then add in other rituals as you grow comfortable with them. Or start with morning and evening devotions, or one only. Concentrate on making your daily practice feel natural, intrinsic to your routine. It is far better to do one thing with your whole heart than to do it all and just go through the motions.

When you have blended one or two activities with your schedule, add something that stretches you a little bit, something you have to work for. You can't learn and grow if you stay in the comfort zone; challenge yourself. Get up a little earlier, forego that extra late-night talk show, turn off the damn cell phone. Remember, nothing worth gaining comes without sacrifice.

Some people will want to rework their lives from the ground up and start cold turkey with a full day's routine of prayer and ritual. While that may work for a few zealous souls, I've found that change is most lasting and most effective when it is accomplished gradually. If a planted acorn shot up to tree height overnight, it probably wouldn't have time to strengthen its trunk and may, in fact, fall over. Learn, again, from nature: take it slowly, and be gentle with yourself. There is no judge, no timekeeper; there is plenty of time to nurture the seeds of your Divine self.

Morning and Evening Devotions

Devotional rituals are a cornerstone of my practice for a number of reasons. First, they help ease the transition from an at-home mindset to a working mindset, making the world of cell phones and traffic jams less jarring to a heart that craves oak trees and *djembe* rhythm. Second, they give me the opportunity to lay my worries in the hands of the Goddess. Problems seem much less pressing when I know I have asked for aid. As a result, devotional rituals teach me to trust in Deity both within myself and without, and to listen for Their advice.

(Notice that I don't intend to hand off my troubles to the Lord and Lady and just expect them to be magically solved. If you've ever thought the gods don't have a sense of humor, just pray for something and then don't get off the couch and work for it. We have free will, two hands, and a mind so we can do our own dirty work.)

A devotional ritual is basically a short, simplified rite that functions like an extended prayer. It attunes you with the elements, then with the Divine, so that you can face whatever comes next with equanimity and grace. While most people won't consistently get out of bed an hour early for aerobics, five or ten minutes to spend with the Lord and Lady in the morning doesn't usually seem so hard to come up with. The ritual itself can be straightforward, with a minimal amount of tools.

Take a look at the morning and evening devotions in the second part of this book, and perhaps give them a try. The words I included are purely optional, of course. Silence is sometimes preferable in ritual, especially first thing in the morning before the coffee's brewed.

This is only one way to go about this sort of ritual. You may want to leave out the elements and stick with Deity alone. I include them in my devotions because I feel our lives crave balance, and this balance can be achieved when we call upon the sacred aspects of our selves. Using the same gestures and themes morning and night will help add a cohesive rhythm to your practice. The most important thing, however, is not to let the words be merely words. Visualize each line clearly. Draw in the attributes of each element, fusing them with your present and future. Imagine that the God and Goddess stand on either side of you, urging you gently into the day ahead or into sleep. For devotions, as in any ritual, you must internalize the action and make it a part of your reality.

If absolute simplicity is a must, or if the best you can do is a minute between your first and second cups of Morning Thunder tea, don't despair. Stand in front of your altar for a moment, take a few deep breaths to clear the clutter and sleep from your mind, and light your prayer candle for a few minutes. Just tell the God and Goddess "Good morning" and let the candle burn while you get dressed. (Don't forget to extinguish it before you leave.) Extend the greeting a bit, making it more poetic if you like, such as, "Bright the day, Blessed Mother and Father; may my every step this day be walked beside You."

Eating with Grace

Almost everyone who has at one time or another dined with a mainstream religious family has experienced mealtime prayer. I remember countless Sundays of "God is great, God is good, let us thank Him for our food. Amen." My brothers and I had an ongoing contest to see who would get in trouble for praying with his eyes open or reaching for a roll before "Amen." It never really occurred to me that something sacred was going on, and years later I regret not paying a little more attention.

Eating is one of the fundamental activities of human existence, and as such it can be a truly beautiful experience. Food and cooking are the alchemy of the elements. The food we eat has passed through many hands, often over many miles, and connects us to others all over the planet. What better way to rejoice in the Earth and all her bounty than to partake of her harvest?

Think about the groceries that come through your kitchen. Bread, for example, is made of the whole planet compounded. The grain grew from dark, rich soil, taking in sunlight and rain. The grain drew close to death, and humans harvested its ripening gold from the fields. Chickens lay eggs, cows gave milk, and more humans ground the wheat into flour. Yet more hands mixed, kneaded, and formed the dough. Fire turned it into bread, searing it the color of sun-dried wheat all over again.

Don't even get me started on yeast.

The point is, that hamburger you ate for lunch is the growth and sacrifice of plants, animals, and humans in an endless dance that nourishes all living things. Before you scarf down your meal without a second thought, it may do you well to give thanks for the lives and loss that went into it, particularly in today's world of factory farming and cruel treatment of livestock.

Many Wiccans I know are vegetarians for precisely that reason, and while I cannot say I blame them, it is a choice each person must weigh for herself. I feel the main reason Americans in particular are willing to let animals suffer as they do is that, to most of us, meat is something that comes wrapped in plastic, not in fur. We have lost our connection to the food we eat and therefore do not honor the creatures it came from. Mealtime prayer is one way to renew this connection. If we could not honor the animal's life, we can at least honor its death.

One interesting side effect of mealtime prayer is that by viewing food as sacred and eating as a religious act, we are much more likely to choose our diet with care. Healthy and organic foods feel much more in tune with the natural rhythms of the Earth than prepackaged, processed items (although there are times when the Twinkie ritual may be in order: "Lord and Lady, we give thanks for this unidentified white goo . . ."). The honest labor of local farmers seems more in keeping with Wiccan spiritual concepts than the antiseptic whirring of machines that clean, cook, and package our food at great waste to the environment. Again, food choices are highly personal, and more factors than religion play into a diet, but at the very least, mealtime prayer will make you more aware of the abundance of the Earth and your role in her abundance. Then the old phrase "saying grace" becomes a perfect description for our wonder and gratitude at the boundless cycle of life.

This can add new dimensions to cooking as well. What is cooking but nourishing others, as the Goddess does us? We become priest or priestess of the kitchen, our actions vital to the well-being of those we love, including ourselves. It's no wonder that a whole tradition of witchcraft revolves around the kitchen. Cooking is one of the oldest forms of magic.

Cleansing the Self

Hopefully, another part of your already-existing routine is bathing in some form or fashion. This, too, is a perfect moment for a mini-ritual. Much has been written about baths as part of spells and rituals, complete with color-coded candles, oils, and music. I suggest something a little simpler, but add to it at will.

When you step into the shower and the water cascades down over you, take a moment to visualize the water washing away all the stress, frustration, and other negative emotions that you have no doubt faced during the day. You can see the negativity as a black film over your skin, or a smell, or whatever fits the way you feel. Regardless, the healing powers of the water sluice off the ick, leaving you clean and renewed. That accomplished, ask silently or aloud to be filled with Divine radiance, then visualize the water becoming just that. It streams down around you, over your entire body, suffusing your skin and hair and very being with soft blue-green light. You could also visualize the light filling and spilling over from your crown chakra downward through the others, then down your legs to the ground.

If a soaking bath is more to your liking, you can do much the same thing. Imagine the negative ick dissolving into the bath where the water destroys it. You may want to drain the water and start fresh, or take a quick shower to rinse off the last of the ick afterward. Alternately, visualize the ick being transformed by the water into a healing energy that soaks back into your skin. Perhaps you might add something to the water—a drop or two of oil, some sea salt, a little milk, or the like—to signify this change.

Once out of the tub, the cleansing need not end. Brushing your teeth can be a way of scrubbing away dishonesty, making room for you to speak the truth, or it can simply bring your attention to the words you say. Getting dressed for any event is comparable to robing for a ritual. You are a priestess donning sacred garb, preparing to walk in the steps of the Goddess. A special piece of jewelry, such as a ring you wear every day, can signify your bond to your gods. When you put it back on after a bath you are "stepping into" your true identity as a Wiccan. The possibilities are endless.

Study and Meditation

In order to further explore the grace of wisdom, you must learn new things. The fact that you are reading this book means you are willing to study at least a little. I encourage you to spend at least a little time every day reading something, whether it's directly relevant to your path or not. Spiritual lessons can come from completely unexpected sources—even trashy novels. Also, if you're trying to plow through a gigantic dry book with eight hundred pages, you might consider keeping something light and fictional nearby to unwind with. Study is an excellent way to make friends with the element of air, which governs intellectual pursuits.

Meditation, too, is a form of study, but instead of learning from an outside source, it encourages you to look within for wisdom. You can meditate on a particular concept—perhaps one you have been reading about—or you can practice a more Zen-like approach. Simply clear your mind, letting thoughts drift through you without attaching yourself to any of them, and let clarity and Divine light settle over you. This takes a lot of patience but is incredibly rewarding. Start slowly—perhaps with ten minutes or so a day—and build up to longer sessions.

I've never been especially good at traditional meditation myself, since my active mind—what Zen Buddhists call Monkey Mind—jumps around like a bonobo on acid. If you have the same problem, you might want to try mantra meditation. Choose a word or a sound, such as the eternal "Om," and repeat it slowly with each breath, extending the sound as far as you can. Mantras, as well as objects to gaze at such as candle flames or symbols, make wonderful focus objects that will help you concentrate long enough to bring your monkey out of its tree.

Ground and Center

One of the most fundamental practices every Wiccan should learn and perform every day is grounding and centering. Most books on Wicca discuss the practice, and with good reason. Grounding reinforces your inherent connection to the Earth, the natural world. Centering reinforces your connection to yourself. Both can be accomplished with the same meditation, and there are many versions of such meditations available.

The most popular version involves visualizing oneself as a tree stretching roots deep into the Earth and branches high into the sky. While this is my favorite being a tree person, there are other versions out there for those who find the tree uninspiring. If you can't find one to your liking, create one. A grounding can be any sort of meditation that makes you feel rooted, strong, and ready. Most involve drawing energy into the body from the Earth, where it gathers in your center and gives you Divine strength and peace. In case you are unfamiliar with the practice, the following is an example.

Find a place where you can sit quietly for a moment with as few distractions as possible. Sit with your back straight and close your eyes. Bring your attention to your breath; try to breathe from deep within your belly, rather than high in your chest. Let your breath lead you into a state of calm, soothing your heartbeat, soothing your mind.

Now imagine yourself sitting in a field of warm, sunlit grass. The sky is a clear, jewel-like blue, the clouds feathery and soft. The breeze kisses your face like an old lover, and you can hear the distant song of birds far off in the forest.

As you exhale, visualize roots extending from your body into the ground. With each breath, send them deeper, passing through the topsoil, through groundwater and bedrock, down through the layers of the Earth. With each breath, your roots draw closer to the center of the Earth, to the heart of the Mother.

Soon, warm Earth energy begins to gather around your roots. Now, as you inhale, draw that energy up through the roots and into your body. Inhale, drawing energy up; exhale, pushing your roots a little deeper. The Earth energy may be colored, or invisible; it may move quickly like electricity or slowly like water. As it fills you, it gives you strength and clarity.

When you feel full of the energy, visualize it pushing out through the top of your head as great spreading branches. With each exhalation, push the branches farther up into the sky, into the clouds, toward the life-giving sun. The sun's gentle heat shines down on your branches, which unfurl their leaves in celebration. Feel your leaves absorbing the sun's energy, the energy of the Father. Each time you inhale, draw it down into your body. The energy mingles with the Earth's energy, turning slowly around the center of your body, where the two mix into a soft white radiance that fills you with peace.

Then, once you are calm and strong and ready, begin to pull your branches and roots back into your body. Inhale, drawing them farther and farther in. When they are fully retracted, imagine that the energy inside you is sealed within your skin. Finally, bring your awareness back to the room you are in, and open your eyes.

Grounding and centering are vital to both your spiritual practice and your magical one, if the two can really be thought of as separate. It should be performed before any ritual or deep meditation, and certainly before casting Circle, but it is also an elegant and simple way to connect to the Divine without tools or ambience. You reach deep into the Mother's essence and up into the Father's realm and draw Them closer, rather like a big meditative hug. Doing a grounding and centering meditation every day will expand your sense of the sacred almost more easily and quickly than any other practice I could suggest. If nothing else, it will leave you open to Their voices and experience.

Exercise

In the previous chapter we discussed the concept of sacred space, but now I want to touch on the most primal and personal sacred space of all: your body. The physical form you have been blessed with is the only one you get this trip, and it is the vehicle through which you experience everything—your senses are all filtered through your body before you can begin to comprehend their messages. In earlier times, people painted their bodies with sacred symbols, colors, and herbs, marking them as children of their gods; people were the ultimate altars.

They still are. No change in your life can take place without your body; you can work no magic without its assistance. Your greatest magical tools are within your skin: hands, heart, mind. Your mouth chants, your feet dance, your spine curves to form the symbols of transformation.

That in mind, how is your temple looking these days? A bit dusty? Neglected? What have you been using to fuel your sacred fire? Cheeseburgers? Some offering!

If the body is an altar, think of all the ways it is used in worship: soothing a child, loving your mate, jogging in the early morning. Your body will tell you when you are treating it like a temple and when you are treating it like an amusement park.

You don't have to be a fitness guru to be kind to your body. In fact, most of the people who fit into today's media image of beauty treat their bodies more like a back alley than a temple: they starve them, slice them open, vacuum them out, work them beyond exhaustion, pump them full of drugs and alcohol. Here's a hint: no matter how many mythology texts you read, you won't find a goddess Bulimia. (If you are a woman trapped in body-image bondage, too afraid of your own fat to move your body, read Maya Angelou's poem "Phenomenal Woman." In fact, copy it into your Book of Shadows this instant.)

To treat your body as the sacred space it is, you have to feed it, move it, breathe in it, and keep it clean. Most of us can manage all but the feeding and moving. We're not stupid; we know what's good for us, and most women I know can quote the exact number of calories in everything they eat. The problem is that we don't think of our physical selves as worthy of the same attention as our minds, which goes back to the Newtonian physics we grew up with in which matter and mind occupy separate realms. We live above the neck.

So get back into your body. Find a way to move it that you enjoy, and no matter what it is, begin with a prayer: "I *dedicate this movement to the Goddess and God, as a prayer in flesh and sweat. Bless this altar, bless my sacred self.*" Your afternoon jog takes on a whole new importance when it's a ritual.

Body Modification

A lot of Pagans—and people in general these days—mark their bodies with tattoos, piercings, and scarification of all kinds to reclaim the physical aspect of their lives as their own. Done in a sacred context, body modification can be a deeply moving experience that forever changes the way you view your skin, but never do any of these things lightly. Be ready to spend a lot of time caring for your tattoo or other mark, helping it heal properly, keeping it free of infection. Also, be very careful what you are invoking by having it permanently drawn on your skin. Viewing the body as holy ground, that Foghorn Leghorn tattoo may be ill-advised.

Case in point: my nineteenth year, just after my birthday, I decided to get my first tattoo. I had absolutely no idea what I wanted; I just knew I had money burning a hole in my pocket and a blank canvas itching for some ink. I wanted to assert my independence as a college girl on her own for the first time, and I wanted to horrify my parents, like any American teenager. Luckily for my aesthetic sensibilities, I chose a fairly tasteful butterfly in a tribal design. Little did I know at the time the butterfly is a symbol of transformation, of rebirth, of remaking your life from the ground up. It is also a symbol of joy; butterflies were thought by some American Indian tribes to carry our prayers to Great Spirit. To get to the joy, however, I had to spend some time in a chrysalis. My life promptly fell apart, and I spent the next few years reassembling myself. I'm glad I did, of course, since the growth and change was beneficial in the long run, but it's still a good example of "Be careful what you don't even know you're wishing for."

(Of course, I have no idea what a Foghorn Leghorn might symbolize, and I'm rather afraid to ask. The moral of the story is: choose body modifications with care.)

Spending Time with Nature

You would think this one would be the easiest. Wicca is a nature religion, after all. So why are 95 percent of rituals done in someone's living room?

Some would say that it's hard to find an outdoor space that's safe anywhere near a city. Good reason. Some would say the neighbors peek over the fence and might call the cops. Another good reason. Others would say mosquitoes in Texas are the size of canaries. True, true.

It's also garbage. It doesn't matter how many Circles you've cast or how many invocations you have memorized, if you can't remember the last time you touched the bark of a tree, felt grass through your fingers, or sang to the moon, you're missing the entire point of Wicca. Nature is our greatest teacher, and no initiation is complete without nature's input.

Dandelions grow in the cracks of inner-city sidewalks. Pigeons nest behind the big neon signs in front of stores. There are even birds living inside your local mall (migration for them must be odd). Nature is everywhere. If you look hard enough, you'll find a natural place that can be your teacher and Divine friend. Cities have parks, botanical gardens, and most importantly, they have roads that go *away* from the cities. Get out in the fields and woods and learn from what you're supposed to revere. Even if all you can manage is once a week for an hour, seek out the trees and rocks and water that live on this planet with you. They have more to say than any human ever has.

Giving to Others

I mentioned service as a part of compassion. One of the surest ways to find the Goddess and God in the world is in the eyes of someone in need, and then in yourself when you give what aid you can. There is always something you can do to be a healing force in your community, from picking up litter in the park to serving soup at a shelter. Everyone has a talent that is useful to the world; being an activist isn't the only way. Try to set aside a little time regularly to give, to embody the Goddess as She pours Her love out on the Earth. Any contribution is a welcome one. Most monasteries these days also run schools, soup kitchens, outreach programs—there's no reason a coven can't do something similar, or an individual. In this day the need for compassion is growing, and one by one, we can help stem the tide.

Even if you are uncomfortable offering direct service to other people, there's almost always something you can do— from clerical work at a charity office to writing letters to your congressperson. If nothing else, donate money. Money is our time and effort in physical, exchangeable form, and is in itself a kind of energy that can be used just as easily to heal as to get you another pair of shoes you'll never wear.

Remember also that humans aren't the only beings that need your help. Animals and the Earth herself could use a little consideration: recycle, carpool, adopt a pet from the local animal shelter, put out a bird feeder in the cold winter months. You may not feel like you've made a substantial contribution, but the birds will beg to differ. Any suffering in the world diminishes us; any healing heals us. Do what you can with what you've got.

The Wiccan at Work

Unfortunately for our sense of the mystical, most of us have to leave our home sanctuaries and spend most of the day in an environment that is uninspiring, to say the least. Work is a necessary part of our modern life, yet almost everyone hates his job or is apathetic toward it. Our jobs support our lives—lives that, for the most part, take place on Saturday and Sunday.

Perhaps we should take a step back and reconsider our outlook on work. Looking at your job, regardless of what it is, how does it help people? How can you, at work, do your job in a way that is healing? Even jobs society considers low on the ladder, including manual labor, can be holy. What is food service but nourishing the bodies of others? Janitorial work is an act of cleansing. If you look hard enough, you can find a redeeming quality in almost any job.

Even if you can't, think of it this way: how can you, as a Wiccan, enrich your working environment? Is there something you can do to make a coworker's life a little brighter? Can you decorate your working space in a way that fosters your spirit? Can you spend your lunch outside among the trees and birds? There is always something, and you do not have to be "out of the broom closet" to be a positive force in the world. If all your job does is bring in money to finance your larger life, it is still a sacred task and may be treated as such.

Develop a ritual for the start of your workday. For instance, at a data entry job I had, I spent most of the day typing what seemed like reams of meaningless numbers. No one would deny my job had very little about it that was spiritual, but every morning when I arrived, my start-up routine had a certain reverence to it. I turned on my computer, got organized, got a cup of coffee. I said a silent prayer that the Lord and Lady would guide my hands and my words, that I would have the strength and calm to act as was fitting a priestess of Their mysteries. The coffee cup was my ritual chalice; the computer was my altar. Unbeknownst to my coworkers, there was a blessing written in a hidden file on the hard drive, and when I put lotion on my hands to stave off paper cuts, I was visualizing my hands as instruments of Divine nurture.

I've known a number of Wiccans who have what you might call "coffee break communion." They sneak out of the office or simply close the door for a few minutes to ground and center, say a brief prayer for the fortitude to finish the workday in an ethical and compassionate manner, or at least bless their aspirin. Even two minutes of fresh air and deep breathing can change your attitude toward the coming afternoon.

The American corporate world is full of unethical people and negative practices, but that doesn't mean our lives need to be. It is possible, with forethought, to carry our ideals into the working world. We only have to be clever, but Wiccans are nothing if not ingenious.

In addition to the work we have to do to finance our lives, there is also our spiritual work. You may not have thought much about it, or ever given it a name. By "work" in this case

I don't mean labor that we do grudgingly for some monetary reward. What do you do that makes you feel connected to Deity? These are things you may have thought of as hobbies, but which, if done with a sacred attitude, can be incredibly meaningful. Do you paint, write, draw, make things? Do you take care of children, garden, walk your dog? Any place you find joy and satisfaction is a place of prayer.

If you don't have any kind of spiritual work at the moment, consider what you would try if you could. There's no time like the present to venture out, take that class, pay off your ten-dollar library fine and read up on Norse mythology or Pablo Neruda or woodworking.

Your interests define your spiritual style—the way you live your path. A logical, linear type may not get much out of painting, but may devour tomes of ancient philosophy. Don't try to force yourself into a model of what you think you should do as a Wiccan. If you live ethically and approach your life as a sacred journey, any kind of activity can be worship—even doing your taxes.

Well, maybe not.

THREE THINGS TO THINK ON

1. When you rise in the morning, become aware of your routine. Does it prepare you for the day? Do you feel energized and inspired when you leave the house? If not, what could you do to help, using any of the ideas from this chapter or anything that comes to mind?

2. Next, consider your work day, your evening. What parts of the day cause you stress, or feel like they need a touch of reverence? What one thing could you do to improve things?

3. When you have arrived at a daily practice that satisfies you, write it out in a sort of "spiritual schedule" in your Book of Shadows or wherever you are compiling your own rule of life. The whole day can be written as a ritual in its own right, a continuous sacred act from dawn to dusk. How do you feel about it?

six

⌐ The Turning Wheel ¬

OUR LIVES ARE A CIRCLE within a circle. Though our spiritual practice happens one day at a time, there are larger spheres that surround us. Days become weeks, become months, become years, and once we have developed a rhythm for the days, it's time to look at the larger picture.

There are many myths attached to the Wheel of the Year. Most of them involve the cycle of the dying and rising God, or the birth and life of the Goddess, or some merger of the two. The God is born to the Goddess and grows into manhood. The two join around Beltane, and as He walks into the Sunset and death, She feels the quickening of a new year in Her belly.

These myths are lovely, and can give texture and richness to the year, but often they become a sort of celestial drama in which the changes of our lives and the seasons become a footnote. Many covens perform the same ritual every Samhain, every Yule, and so on.

Repetition in ritual has value, of course, especially in the context of the Wheel. It helps us to see that whatever happens on a small scale, the Earth renews herself each year just as she has every one before and will for years to come. However, no two years can ever be the same in a human's life. Even the environment changes with each turning, as animals and plants die and make way for new growth. Performing the exact same ritual from one Imbolc to the next is not only boring, it shows a lack of personal growth. As we grow and change, so should our practice, and the sabbats are a perfect opportunity to reflect our evolution.

Another problem with the Wheel as it is currently celebrated is that, for the majority of the community, the Wheel of the Year only seems to happen eight times a year. Never mind that there are 357 other days, and that the seasons don't change right on schedule at equinoxes. The Wheel turns slowly, gradually, with each season fading into the next. The Wheel doesn't stop on each sabbat and wait for us to have a party. It is continuous, moving as we speak.

What does the Wheel of the Year mean to you? Have you learned to notice the subtle changes in the world around you, and within you, as the seasons move along?

I live in Austin, Texas, which has a large and diverse Pagan community. One thing I have noticed, with no end of amusement, is that the vast majority of Wiccan books that deal with the Wheel do so from a northern, or European, perspective. I attended a Yule ritual once in which the priestess recited a beautiful invocation to the Goddess that mentioned

"Her winter mantle of glistening white" and "the snow that lies soft and deep."

I've lived in Texas all my life and never seen more than half an inch of snow. In fact, on December 21 of that year it was about sixty degrees Fahrenheit.

Unfortunately, it doesn't occur to a lot of Wiccans that the nature we're supposed to revere is the nature *where we live*, not some abstract ideal of winter or summer or whatever. If it never gets below fifty degrees in your climate, it might be a good idea to rethink Yule.

Just because Wiccans over in England do a Spiral Dance on the summer solstice, it doesn't mean you're obligated, especially if it's so hot half your Circle would drop from heat stroke halfway through.

Don't misinterpret me; tradition is very important. It connects us with all those who have gone before, and all those all over the world who share our beliefs and values. It's our common practices and ideals that give us community and continuity from generation to generation. However, our religion is one of the Earth, and it must reflect the Earth under our feet. As a society we are disconnected from our surroundings; as Wiccans we must reconnect in order to touch the sacred.

I suggest you find a place out in nature—a spot you can return to frequently—and follow it for a year. Go there periodically—not just on the sabbats, but in between—and observe how the seasons have altered it. Start where you are in the cycle. Write down or sketch what you see and how it changes, and also what changes have occurred in yourself. Notice how the two intersect. Western civilization has sundered itself from the seasons; we live in artificial environments that upset the natural rhythms of our bodies. Once you begin to realign your heart with the outside world, you will notice that the year's waxing and waning has a gentle but definite effect on you as well.

Beyond any myths, beyond the human-imposed structure of holidays and festivals, lies the true Wheel of the Year. Forget every book you've read, everything you've been told. Forget what our supposedly Pagan ancestors did on each holiday, and what the days meant to them. Forget everything you know about the Wheel, and go out and learn the seasons from the seasons themselves.

A MEDITATION ON THE WHEEL OF THE YEAR

This meditation was written in September, but really you can begin at any season and follow it back around. I recommend you go to your special place outdoors to read it, and spend some time reaching out with your senses, acquainting yourself with the season you are in right now before you move on. What does the air feel like around you, and how is it different from the last time you were outside? What does a change of season mean to the place you are at?

The point of this meditation isn't so much that it will line up exactly with your climate; where you live may very well be the opposite of where I live. The words that follow, however, will hopefully inspire you to go deep into the land around you and truly experience the Wheel of the Year the way our ancestors likely did—as a dynamic, primal force of change that influences our very cells.

This is autumn, the season of water, the season of letting go.

The leaves are tired, heavy on the branches from a long summer of heat and growth. Fruit hangs ready and swollen on the vine. There is a quiet to the world—a waiting, a listening for the first chill winds to bluster down from the north.

In the woods around you, the animals can sense the coming of colder weather. The squirrels gather in all the food they can, knowing that this is their own time of harvest. The deer test the wind more carefully now, as hunting season is coming, just as it did last year and the year before. Some of them will fall; they always do. They spent the summer learning to be quick, to blend in. Now all their knowledge will protect them as the humans enter the forest.

Autumn is the evening of the year, the sunset. The light is waning but not gone; the heat is lessening but not absent. The time of harvest can mean many things. What has been sown must now be reaped, for better or worse. It is the time of elderhood—of Mother giving way to Crone, of staring down into the darkness of death and waiting, waiting for the moment to jump. As such it is the season of water—of emotion, of release, of the tears of letting go our mistakes and successes before the year has ended and it is time to start anew.

Autumn is the time to take stock, to bring in the harvest for the cold to come. The trees conserve their strength, withdrawing support from their leaves to keep the trunk alive through winter. The leaves let go of the branches and drift to the ground with a sigh, a final breath before rejoining the Earth. Autumn is that last breath.

Soon the days grow cooler, the air a little lighter. Fewer and fewer animals venture out. Around you, many trees stand stripped bare, skeletal, their true shape showing through. Some, the evergreens, brace themselves for the change in temperature, whatever it may be. The plants and animals in this wood already know how cold it will get. They are blessed with an instinct that we have forgotten: to know in advance what kind of winter to plan for. Their fur has grown shaggy, their bark has thickened, all in accordance with their knowledge of the earth. New birds appear from the upper climates, in search of the milder cold this land can offer.

The rains come again, as they did at autumn's onset, but now they are chilly. Your breath begins to catch in the air, smoking like a dragon's. For some creatures it is a time to burrow deep and sleep; for others, the cold is energizing, and they run through the trees leaving tracks in the mud. Predators stay low to the ground, waiting in the underbrush for one who has grown careless with relief from summer's oppressive heat.

This is winter, the season of earth, the season of survival and death. The Earth itself is naked, her skin bare to the cold winds as the plants die back and the trees give up their last few leaves. Everything is exposed, vulnerable, and the focus of life becomes getting through one day at a time. Questions hang in the air:

"Did anyone hear that?"

"Is it safe?"

"Is there enough?"

In winter, time seems to slow down, and the days—though shorter—are a struggle in the wild. Every day a hundred battles are waged between predator and prey, and in winter the predator often wins. We hide, hunker down in the long shadows, and rub our hands together for warmth.

The nights are a crystalline wonder of stars and endless black skies; outlines are sharper, our senses are heightened. Death extends a hand, inviting us to step out of the battered body of the old year and walk toward the new. We shed our skins, leaving ourselves as open as the Earth, and rely on the strength and knowledge we gained during the past turning to help us stay on our feet.

The winter, though, cannot last. Death can never keep a hold on life for more than a little while; Death is a gateway, not an end. It nudges us gently forward, reluctant but understanding, and we step through the gate into air that is ever so slightly warmer, a little heavier, with the scent of flowers almost like a distant memory.

Around you, a few tentative green shoots have pushed up through the hard soil. A deer pokes her head out of the underbrush, hopeful. Tiny buds have appeared on the tips of branches overhead. The wind still blows with a chill, but something has altered— something subtle and promising.

This is spring, the season of air, the season of renewal. Each dawn brings a warmer morning, and the air itself whispers of rebirth. Blossoms, babies, ideas—it is all one to the air. A beginning is a beginning. The Earth takes a great breath in, lets it out slowly, and stretches stiff limbs before rising.

We feel a sudden need to slough off what remains of the past, to cleanse ourselves and our surroundings. It's time to make way for what will grow in the new year; to till the fertile ground of our lives and sow our dreams. The seeds that have waited, dormant, throughout the winter are now pushing down and up, roots and shoots, bursting through the ground and heralding their arrival with a fanfare of green and gold.

The bare ground is now alive with a riot of pastels. The urge to leap, run, and play infects all the young of all the creatures. Overhead, baby squirrels chatter while their parents streak from branch to branch in noisy celebration that spring is here at last. As the days lengthen, new animals rise from the thicket on wobbly legs and totter around, getting a first taste of the warm air and endless beauty of the Earth.

The season of air is one of inspiration, of new plans, and the energy of a deep breath. Air carries the music of creation, of renewal; it carries the song of birds and the laughter of children. The young begin to learn, their minds reaching out along with their oversized puppy paws. Spring is the morning of the year: a time to yawn, look around, and get ready.

Gradually, slowly, one day at a time, the air grows hotter. The sun's radiant eye opens wider and wider, and the freshness becomes heaviness. Blossom turns to bud turns to fruit, and the fruit swells on the branches. Plan turns to action, and the pastels deepen into wild shades of green and gold.

This is summer, the season of fire, the season of motion and energy. Life breaks free; it will not be denied. Eating and mating and playing in the fields are all that matters under the sun. The trees show off their finery: leaves fluttering in the wind and taking in the light. The world around you reaches a fever pitch, and the Earth almost seems to turn faster. One pair of eyes meets another across a forest glade, and fire builds between them.

The wind is singing love ballads—with the birds in accompaniment—as relationships form and strengthen. Mother to child, brother to sister, lover to lover—fire binds them all.

The afternoons stretch out lazily, satisfied, as the animals sun themselves with full bellies and contented minds. There is plenty for all in the summer, no need to fight or scramble; abundance grows all around. The air is hot, but the trees give welcome shade, and for a moment there is nothing wanting, no reason to worry. One day blends gently into another, and the sun rises higher.

The days, though, will not be comfortable for long. The heat begins to build, unrelenting, as late summer beckons. The heaviness of previous days is oppressive now—the air thick, blanketing the woods with silence and stillness. The animals seek shelter from the sun, and the frenetic pace of life comes almost to a halt, tired from its exertions. Fire begins to yield once more to water, as the consequences of our actions bring forth sweat and sometimes tears. Now is the gathering-in of strength, the watchful eye on the fields. Harvest is coming, and the plants have grown to their fullest.

A silence, the pause between breaths—then the first cool winds start to blow, and the Wheel turns round again.

The Elemental Wheel

If you lay a compass over the Wheel of the Year, you find another of the many Wiccan mysteries. The elements, the directions, and the sabbats are deeply connected. The meditation above shows a little of how the seasons and the elements line up. Let's look at it again in the context of the sabbats.

DAYS OF WATER: MABON AND SAMHAIN

Water is the element of *flow*. It carves away at the tallest mountains and carries the sediment of time to the sea. It is also the element of emotion, memories, and of letting go. In the autumn, facing the end of the year and the hard days of winter not far ahead, we must choose what to hold on to and what to let the tide wash away. We bless the events that have brought us to where we are, then let them go.

Water in the atmosphere moves in a continuous cycle, from cloud to ground and back again, and so is a reminder of the cyclical nature of life. In agricultural societies, much time is spent during one season preparing for the next, and similarly in autumn we must look ahead to the barren time.

At Mabon, we pause to give thanks for all the moments of the previous year, both good and bad, and the lessons we have learned. It is a chance to take stock of our personal harvest—the consequences of our actions—and then let them pass away into the stream. Water teaches us that nothing stays forever; we have to release our emotions or they will stagnate and poison us. We hold on to the memories that will help us survive the coming seasons, but we cannot let them hold on to us.

The plants around us have ripened and, once harvested, begin the journey toward death. The birds head south, or, if we live in southern climes, new birds arrive. Children return to school, with only the memory of their carefree summer days remaining.

In the great Wheel of Life, Mabon is the time of elderhood, of turning within for the wisdom we have gathered throughout our lives. We aren't ready to take the final step into death just yet, but we feel its chill presence and must make peace with it.

Then, Samhain is here, and darkness falls. Traditionally Samhain is a time of divination, of communicating with absent friends or the deepest parts of ourselves, the still silent waters in our spirits. Our own ghosts, our personal demons, come back to haunt us. The water of Samhain is motionless, reflective, and we can look into its mirrored surface and see all the mysteries that lay beyond life. At Samhain, the past year finally slips away, and with one last breath we close our eyes . . . only to open them again, at another time, another place, another life.

Water is usually associated with the west, the land of sunset, and Samhain is the moment when the sun's last rays disappear behind the horizon and twilight drops its misty veil. We can look behind the veil and see things that were hidden by the light of day. The Crone steps forward, leaning heavily on her cane, and the knowledge of death is in her eyes.

DAYS OF EARTH: YULE AND IMBOLC

Earth stands still, silent, waiting. It is the body, wrapped tightly in coats and blankets against the frigid air of winter. It is the silhouette of the trees, the track of a wolf in snow or mud. It is the element of the physical, and in winter it is concerned with survival.

Even if you live in a mild climate, winter is still a time to stay close to the safety and comfort of home. Traditional holidays during winter are those that encourage family gatherings, coming together around the hearth fire. The sounds and smells of this season are those things that endure: evergreens, the scent of your mother's baking pies, the sound of family in the next room. Earth hides the roots of plants, and in winter we seek out our own roots for comfort, fellowship, and rest.

At Yule—the moment of greatest darkness—we experience true stillness. Yule is the pause between one life and another; a time to consider what choices we will have to make before rebirth. The forest is quiet, the fields are bare. In winter we can see the shapes hidden beneath outer form. Even your breath hangs in the air.

Earth, though, is not always barren. It holds limitless potential, and thus so does winter. Eventually something changes, and the ground beneath us stirs. Even with Yule's cold hand still covering the land, we begin to make plans. What will the coming year bring? What will the seeds that lie dormant beneath the soil grow into?

The wisdom of our bodies speaks to us as winter turns toward spring, and we feel the first sparks of energy in our muscles. Imbolc is here, the Festival of Light. A candle shines in the window, guiding us through the now-waning dark, and we start to look ahead.

Earth is the element of manifestation, and in order to manifest something, you first have to know what you want. At Imbolc, the Wheel is halfway between earth and air, and as air is the element of thought, Imbolc is a time to think things through while we wait.

Imbolc is a time to sweep away the last of the cobwebs of the old year, and often we find ourselves attacking our homes with a broom. As we do away with the dust, we wonder what to do with the space once it's clean. Imbolc is preparation, consideration. Nothing has happened yet, and we aren't quite ready to put our plans into motion, but we have plenty of time waiting for the winter to draw to a close. As the Earth reminds us, there is always time.

DAYS OF AIR: OSTARA AND BELTANE

Breathe!

Air is beginning, the east, where the sun rises. Spring is the sunrise of the year; renewal is its watchword. Inspiration flies free with the warming breezes. It may still be cold where you live, but there is a wonderful and subtle current in the weather that whispers, "Spring has sprung..."

Ostara has long been the sabbat of rebirth, even as appropriated by Christianity. Eggs and bunnies abound. As the equinox, Ostara marks a brief period of balance leaning toward the light. All things are possible, and probability runs high; the vitality of the Earth has returned, and so has our own. We strip off our heavy coats and start new projects. It is a time of great creativity, as air is the element of the imagination and of exploration. New pursuits and ideas are all of the air. As the birds hatch their eggs, we hatch our plans.

The time of renewal is the time of childhood, of stretching our legs. The world is so new, so alive, we strain to take it all in. Ostara reflects our childhood innocence and thirst to learn and grow.

The air warms further still, and so do our hearts. Air influences all realms of communication, and the older we get, the more we need to communicate. As Beltane comes around, we have reached adolescence—the time of "Notice me!" The fertility of spring reaches a fever pitch. Beltane lands on the Wheel halfway between air and fire, and that much is evident from the number of couples that head off into the corn fields after the bonfire on Beltane Eve.

Beltane is a time of freedom—both from our cares and from the constraints of society—and it reflects the yearning for independence that marks young adulthood. It is all about relationships, the way lovers and friends and species relate to each other, which harkens back to the airy power of communication. With air—which is essentially empty, but carries sound and scent and spirit—whipping all around us, we can expect some miscommunication to occur, particularly with the emerging influence of fire just around the corner.

DAYS OF FIRE: LITHA AND LAMMAS

Fire, of course, is the element of passion and drive. As the Wheel turns toward summer, our plans become action, and we undertake the task of turning our ideas into reality with gusto. The atmosphere heats up and we pounce—on our dreams, on the future, on each other.

Litha, the summer solstice, is the longest day. The year has built power all this while, and now it sends that power out into the universe to do its will. The scents of green growing things and herbs drying in the sun stir our senses. Litha is a time of amazing bounty—the zenith of the year, high noon. It is a time of action—of doing, not simply being—and a time of the leap of faith. Action is always tempered by tension, as action can lead just as easily to failure as to success.

Litha marks the end of the waxing half of the year, as from this moment onward the days will begin to grow shorter as we progress toward autumn. Therefore it is almost a frenzy of movement, of incredible brightness and exuberance—a last dance.

In southern climates, the heat builds and builds until it becomes almost unbearable. Once the Midsummer's dances are done, we run for the shade. The crops ripen under the sun, and the Earth bakes. The first fruits are ready, and from their taste we can get some idea of what the harvest will hold. Things start to move more slowly as the heat tires everyone out, and with Lammas on the horizon, we take a deep breath and stretch our weary limbs.

Lammas, the first harvest, is the harvest of grain. Wheat, corn, and other grains are the first crops to ripen every year, and therefore the first to sacrifice themselves for our nourishment. Within each grain is the future—without the harvest, nothing will grow next year. Fire is the element of sacrifice, as it must consume something in order to live. Our lives and our dreams do not come without cost, and Lammas is a reminder that in order to ensure the future, we must be ready to face, conquer, and release the past. It also reminds us that although the fruits of our labor have started to come in, we cannot rest on our laurels just yet. There is still more work to do before the year is done.

In this fiery time of year, the transforming nature of that element makes itself known. Flower turns to fruit, the fruit is harvested, and the seeds become the hope for the next plant. We transform grain into bread—indeed, Lammas is known to many as the Festival of Bread. In our lives, Lammas is the time of maturity, when we must transform ourselves into whoever it is we are to become. In this time of abundance, we are already thinking about the autumn, and the next harvest that isn't far away.

One interesting exercise I recommend to anyone who wants to become more attuned to the seasons is to draw out a Wheel of the Year diagram and superimpose the months of the calendar year on it. Add on your birthday and any significant anniversaries. Then, go back through the last year and start penciling in the events of the year—both good and bad—that you considered significant. You could even do this for two or three years if your memory is that good. Try to fill it in as completely as possible—include everything from deaths and births in your family to new jobs, new pets, large purchases, new projects, completed goals, and journeys made. Add in important events in the larger world, both in the Pagan community and the global one. Also consider how your health and emotional well-being fluctuate.

You may not see any kind of patterns in this Wheel, but don't worry, this year is sort of a background layer. Now, make another Wheel, and start with the current year up to the point you're at as you read this.

As the year goes on, and you work to become closer to Deity and to nature, keep track of where the events of your life fall on the Wheel. Spend time outdoors in the place you have chosen to observe the seasons, and try to bring more nature into your life in general as part of your daily practice. It may even take a few years to show any correlation. As I said, we are as a society largely divorced from nature, and reconnecting ourselves will probably not be an overnight process.

THREE THINGS TO THINK ON

1. Which of the sabbats do you enjoy celebrating the most? Which have little meaning to you? Look at them in the context of the elements, and see how they relate to where you are in your life right now.

2. When you spend time in your chosen outdoor spot, keep a journal of the weather and other conditions, the animals you see, and the changes in the place. Also keep note of what's going on in your life each time you visit. Do you notice any connections? If not, does your life at least seem to run in a cycle of some kind? Are you in a particular ele-

mental phase right now? Does water rule you, or air? Keep track of these observations as well.

3. If you could add a sabbat to the Wheel of the Year (or several), what would it celebrate?

seven

The Dance of Life

THE LAST THING I WANT to talk about with you is the idea of personal tradition and ritual. By this, I mean the rituals you create yourself that honor your own life, whether they are yearly traditions or once-in-a-lifetime events. A variety of topics fall under this category, and the first is a method for creating your own rituals.

There are a handful of traditional rites of passage that get a lot of attention in ritual books: handfastings, Wiccanings, menarche rites, funerals, and so forth. These milestones, however, are only a very few of the myriad moments we have to celebrate in our lives. Rituals help us declare and understand the importance of these occasions.

Very often, the events that truly define us are glossed over and pass by without notice, either because they aren't socially demarcated "holidays," or because we don't realize their significance ourselves. When you become aware of the sacred nature of all life, however, little things begin to take on a new vitality, and you develop a desire to mark these definitive occasions with at least a momentary, personal observance.

Think back to the things that have happened in your life that ended up being instrumental in making you the person you are today. Were any of them celebrated, or did they get swept under the rug of everyday routine? How would you have felt and lived differently if those moments had been given their due recognition?

That's what personal rites of passage—and indeed, all personal rituals—are about: noticing and acknowledging our defining moments and their inherent holiness. That new job or failed relationship may have seemed mundane at the time, but it changed you on some level or you wouldn't remember it.

Creating personal rituals is one of the most important, and most often overlooked, aspect of Wicca. There are several books already in existence on the subject, but they can be rather daunting to someone who is used to using prewritten material. As vital as ritual is to our practice, a great many of us don't feel at all confident in our creative abilities, and a lot of books make the process so complicated it becomes intimidating instead of inspiring. That leaves us with prewritten rituals, and while these may be lovingly crafted by sincere authors, they are still not our own. I have rarely come across a ritual in someone else's words that I didn't need to change at least a little bit to fit my needs.

Apart from the creation of sacred space, rituals themselves are not terribly complicated. They all have a set of essential elements, and whatever window dressing and decoration you add to them can be as complex as you like. Pared down to its most basic steps, creating ritual consists of the following:

1. The idea
2. The action
3. The stuff

The Idea

Okay, why are you doing this ritual? It may seem like a rhetorical question, but you'd be surprised how many people get halfway through a ritual without having any idea why they're there. I've been to plenty of beautifully orchestrated rites without a point. For example, I attended a public ritual during one year in which Beltane fell on the full moon, and after the Circle was opened, I couldn't figure out whether they'd been trying to hold a sabbat or an esbat, if either. The metaphors were so muddled you couldn't be certain one way or the other. Did "great shining orb" mean the moon or the sun?

The reason for your ritual doesn't have to be big and dramatic. "I just wanted to celebrate life" and "I got health insurance" are perfectly valid premises. The important thing is to have an intention—something you're trying to accomplish.

There are three basic purposes in ritual. The first is *invocation*. You want to gain something, to get something started, to bless something or some event that has passed or may yet occur. This kind of ritual often involves magic—raising energy to effect a certain positive outcome—or it can simply be a calling for best wishes and smooth sailing.

The second purpose is *banishing*, when there is something in your life that no longer serves your personal growth. This also includes marking the end of a relationship, severing its ties to your heart, or actively working to get a certain someone out of your life. While manipulating people's lives is against Wiccan precept, we can hardly be expected to keep up relationships with people who drain our energy or make us unhappy. I suppose it would be more appropriate to say that we banish the relationship instead of the person.

The third purpose, and the most joyful, is simply *celebration*. Sabbats can fall into this category, as can rites of gratitude—whether it's to say "Thank you," "Thank goodness that's over," or "I made it! Yahoo!"

The purposes can be mingled, such as an Ostara ritual during which you ask a blessing on some new project or a Samhain that involves banishing a negative situation that has recently arisen. It's best, however, to keep your idea as simple and straightforward as possible. You can layer symbols and activities on top of your intention, but the more ingredients there are in your gumbo, the more likely it is that something will taste funny. Try to condense your ritual's premise into ten words or less.

Be careful, though, that you are clear on the real motivation behind your ritual. Often we fix our attention on a symptom of a problem, when the disease itself continues unchecked in our psyches. The most common example I have seen is when people try to repair damaged self-esteem by working magic to find a lover or lose weight, thereby ignoring the forest for the trees. Three failed relationships and twenty pounds later, they are still filled with self-loathing, and often do even more magic, slapping a bandage on the outer wound while ignoring the one that's still bleeding.

One time-honored and frequently overlooked method of discerning our hidden motivations is divination. Whatever your preferred form of divination is, consult it to see if the cards or runes or whatever can give you some insight into what it is you really need at this point in your life. You may be surprised. Divination is incredibly useful in poking into the corners of ourselves that we don't or would rather not see. It is an avenue for communication between ourselves, our subconscious minds, and the Divine. If you don't have a personal oracle that you consult, now may be the time to start learning one.

The Action

Now that you have an idea, and it's clear to you why you're stepping into the Circle, you have to have something to do with it. Rituals are symbolic in nature, relying on the principle of "like attracts like," so the action you come up with should reflect your deepest emotional response to the intention you've formed.

When you think about the subject matter, what's your gut reaction? What does your body and heart want to do with it? For example, suppose you want to do a ritual severing your ties to an ex-lover. How do you feel about this person? Angry?

Tired? Afraid? What does your body want to do with those feelings? Bury them? Burn them? Cut them into little pieces? Put them on ice?

How do those feelings translate into action? You could take the ex's picture and bury it at the base of a tree, hoping to transform your negative feelings about him into something living and healing. If he was abusive, burning the picture to burn away his influence over you may be appropriate. If all you desire is independence, consider cutting yourself out of the picture and destroying the ex's half, praying that he will move on and let you both find a better place for your affections.

Banishing is fairly easy to orchestrate, but what about invocation? Perhaps you are starting a new project—say, writing a book. You might create a small model of whatever it is you're doing and empower it as a representation of the finished product. You could plant seeds that will grow as your project grows. Or you could simply light a candle and express your hopes and fears, asking the Lord and Lady to help you find the strength and clarity you know you will need to accomplish your goals.

There are many sources of inspiration for ritual actions. The four elements can be of great help, especially when it comes to ritual magic. Consider your intention for a moment, and what element or elements it relates to most strongly. How can that element help you?

Earth rituals involve physical things, such as survival, career, health, and fertility. Earth is the element of manifestation, of material objects and possessions, but also of the rhythms of life and the body. If you need help moving from one phase of life to another, earth can help you listen to the heartbeat of change. Bury things, plant seeds, or create symbolic objects out of clay or stones.

Water rituals are healing, flowing, and feminine. Any ritual involving women's mysteries, childbirth, or gentle change are sympathetic to water. One delightful ritual I helped with had all the practitioners draw symbols of healing on the sidewalk with chalk, which an impending rainstorm carried away to the gods. Water is most often a loving element, though if you've been in a flash flood, you know how it can rage. It represents the wide gamut of our emotions.

Fire rituals are all about transformation: destruction, creation, banishing, rising from the ashes. Most of us have had some experience—both positive and negative—with fire energy. The warmth of a hearth or the terror of a forest blaze, fire consumes what it touches and changes it forever. Anything involving passion, anger, and the shedding of old skin can involve fire.

Air rituals involve the mind. Imagination, laughter, music, communication—if it has words or sound, it's air-related. Air is the scholar's friend and the writer's muse. Air follows us from first breath to last, and brings renewal on each inhalation. It is the hardest element to hold on to, but the most fundamental to our existence. Play music, burn incense, and *breathe*.

Of course, you can play with the correspondences a little, depending on the nature of your desire. There are, for instance, all kinds of love. If you want to love yourself and overcome body image issues, earth would be your element. If you want smiley, hearts-and-flowers, romantic love, go with water. If you want hot monkey love, try fire. Creating something can involve all four elements: first comes the idea, in air; then comes the emotions attached to that idea, in water; then comes the desire and drive to create, in fire; then comes the actual manifestation of your idea, in earth.

Another place to look for ritual action is in mythology. Does your situation remind you of a story you've read, a god or goddess you studied once? What did he or she do in that story that you could repeat in some fashion? There have been myriad rituals involving Persephone or the descent of Inanna, but the wealth of myths our ancestors left us can be applied to all sorts of situations. If you revere a specific form of Deity, did his or her myths relate to your intention?

Artemis is a virgin goddess, meaning independent and whole unto Herself as opposed to the modern definition of "virgin." According to Greek myth, each year She bathed in a sacred spring to renew Her purity and cleanse Herself of the influence of men. I translated this evocative idea into a ritual of personal purification after a particularly horrific incident, hoping to reclaim the power of my womanhood.

A friend of mine used the descent of Inanna as inspiration for her Samhain ritual. But instead of going through the entire myth cycle, she simply had the attendees remove their outer layers of clothing and hang them on a tree, symbolic of the time the Goddess spent hanging on a hook in the Underworld.

Another Wiccan I know created a dance ritual to the god Dionysus to celebrate newfound joy. Another grieved the loss of her husband with the help of Isis and Osiris. The possibilities are endless, as human myths reflect the universal experiences of humankind.

The wonderful thing about finding your inspiration in mythology is that such ideas give you an instant connection to the Divine in your ritual. The story itself will tell you the symbols, tools, words, and decorations you could use. In the Artemis ritual I mentioned, I used a lot of lunar symbolism and the color white, which is associated with purification. I had white candles everywhere, and I bathed by their light, adding milk and white rose petals to my bath. Artemis is also associated with the hunt, so I placed a figure of two white deer near the tub. You can do quite a bit of research into the symbols and culture of the story that speaks to you and incorporate that into your rite.

Be sure you at least have a good handle on the story itself so that you're invoking what you want to invoke. I heard a rather telling story about a Wiccan who created a ritual around the story of the Norse god Odin, who was given the gift of occult knowledge and the first runic alphabet. The Wiccan in question was seeking to gain similar knowledge, not acknowledging that in order to gain it, Odin had hung upside down from the World Tree for nine days (nothing comes without sacrifice). After losing most of his possessions in a house fire and nearly dying himself, the Wiccan developed the ability to read the runes with uncanny accuracy. He has been a lot more careful with mythology since then.

The action is often the biggest stumbling block for people learning to create rituals. When in doubt, seek help! There are dozens of books in print that contain rituals, and the best way to learn the process is by studying and picking apart extant rituals. If you're planning a full moon ritual, look at a few prewritten esbats and see what about them appeals to you. Everyone has his own ritual style, so some kinds of rites will resonate with you and some won't. You may lean toward the ceremonial, or toward a more spontaneous and free-flowing type—the only way to know is to try them out. How could you incorporate ideas from other sources into your own? Be certain, if you're in a group, to give credit to the sources you borrowed from. If you put a patchwork-style ritual into your own Book of Shadows, make a note of where the parts came from. It's the ethical thing to do, and it will help you remember where to look if someone asks, "Great invocation. Where did you get it?"

The Stuff

The last consideration in creating a ritual is the practical side: the stuff. What tools do you need? How will you decorate your altar and the space around it? Where will the ritual be held? How many people will attend, or is it private? The objects and sensual experiences you use in ritual will add more meaning to your actions and help you focus your intention.

Also, is there a particular time of the day, week, month, or year you feel you should perform the rite? Correspondences for timing abound in Wiccan texts. Timing isn't everything, but doing a ritual for banishing with the waning moon can add another layer of symbolic meaning and effectiveness to the ritual.

Some rituals are most meaningful with no tools at all, particularly those held out in the wild under a full moon or in some other place that is naturally sanctified. Often, all that is needed is you. Rituals performed at home in the living room, though, generally need more toys and more atmosphere.

If you think of a ritual as a person, then the idea is its heart. The action is its body, allowing it to move around and accomplish the purpose its heart holds. The stuff, then, is the clothing that the ritual wears, and depending on its purpose, location, and planned activities, it will dress differently. Some will go naked; others will have on a full panoply of robes, tools, and jewelry. It all depends on what's in the ritual's heart.

Reasons to Rite

In case you are still stumped about creating your own rituals, I've come up with a fairly long list of reasons why you might want to give it a try. Some of these reasons may seem extremely minor, but meaning is in the eye of the beholder. Hopefully this list will spark off some ideas for you, or at least give you a place to start looking.

I'm starting a job hunt.
I found a new job.
I got a promotion.
I paid off my student loans.

I got into grad school.

I dropped out of college.

It's the start of a school year.

It's the end of a school year.

I'm setting a goal.

I've achieved a goal.

I'm trying to find inspiration for a new project.

I'm trying to finish a new project, but I've hit a wall.

I'm done with my project and good riddance!

I'm learning a new [spiritual or other] discipline.

I'm looking for a new car.

I'm blessing a new [car/house/piece of furniture/magical tool/piece of jewelry].

I got a new pet.

I lost a pet.

I'm searching for a lost pet.

I lost a relative.

I gained a relative (birth/marriage/adoption).

It's the end of a friendship (on good terms or bad).

It's the end of a romantic relationship.

It's the end of an abusive relationship (banishing).

My ex didn't get the house or the kids.

My ex got twenty to life.

I'm declaring my personal independence.

I'm ready to love again.

I need to get out more (expanding my circle of friends).

I want to [start/join/escape] a coven.

I survived violence.

I survived a [tornado/earthquake/visit from in-laws/car accident/root canal].

I [recovered/will recover] from illness or injury.

I am cleansing my home after a [break-in/disaster].

I'm returning from a journey.

I'm embarking on a journey.

I'm looking for a new home.

I have found a new home.

I'm leaving an old home.

I'm bidding farewell to emotional baggage.

Lord give me strength.

My kids have moved out.

My kids have moved back in.

There was an [earthquake/terrorist attack/plane crash/car bomb] in the world and I want to do something.

Let my life be a candle to help dispel darkness.

My inner child needs milk and cookies.

[I/My household] needs purification.

I want to [dedicate/rededicate] myself to a religious path.

I [changed a tire/fixed the toilet/did my taxes] for the first time.

Hey, it's Tuesday!

A Many-Gendered Thing

I had not really intended to devote much space to the idea of gender mysteries. As a woman, I don't feel at all qualified to talk about men's rituals, and I feel there are more than plenty of books on women's rituals by now.

Then I had a face-to-face confrontation with just how twisted our images of gender, power, and sexuality have become in modern society, and I changed my mind. The details are unimportant; suffice it to say I was attacked in a place and time I had mistakenly thought was safe and sacred, and it tore my conviction of the basic goodness of people up one side and down the other. Once the bruises were healed and the nightmares started to fade, I began to regain my optimism, but I had to admit that the incident left me with a new understanding of how deeply ingrained and far-reaching the wounds of society are.

Men are taught from an early age that the way to gain power is to take it and batter people with it until they get their way, whether in business, sex, or family relationships. They are forced to suppress their emotions, both positive and negative, and squeeze themselves into a box that is just as narrow and confining as the one set out for women. It goes even deeper than the old "boys don't cry" sentiment; anger and frustration are just as frowned upon as grief. Women are encouraged to be assertive, to learn to play the game in a "man's world," and thereby become more like men to reach their goals while giving up their essential femininity. Men, however, aren't even supposed to act like their own stereotype, as being a "typical male" is just as socially stigmatized today as being a "sissy."

Perhaps in the past, the men in control of society were by and large responsible for the oppression of women, and perhaps women contributed to their own oppression by buying into the stereotypes—that isn't the point. The point is that now, in a time when gender roles are more fluid than ever, we have to recognize that both sexes are hurt and in need of healing, and the only way to achieve true equality is to work on both.

We live in a universe of Divine complements, where "opposing" forces and their attraction to each other drive the Dance of Life. Light and dark, positive and negative, masculine and feminine—all cannot exist without each other. Women's mysteries without men's mysteries are incomplete. While women are off planning elaborate menarche rites for pubescent girls, what are the men doing? Just as women don't want to be pigeonholed into cooking and making babies, there is more to masculine life than football and belching contests.

In Wicca, men often get the short end of the wand, and so does the God. That is understandable, as the largest percentage of Wiccans is women, and at times, the menfolk are in short supply. Women have found a haven in Wicca, at last finding a religion that affirms their rights, desires, and bodies. The idea of feminine Deity is so inspiring, so amazing, that the masculine is shoved off into "Yeah-He-already-has-plenty-of-holidays" land. Even worse, many women feel so beaten down by the gods of their childhood that the Wiccan God becomes a new face on an old unwelcome guest, and they'd rather have an unbalanced tradition than stare down their old conditioning and create new images of masculinity.

I was Dianic for several years, so I know firsthand how difficult it is to let go of the patriarchal, abusive, father god to embrace Someone else. God had ignored me for most of my life, and here was the Goddess, Her arms open wide and Her eyes dancing with the delight of finding Her wayward daughter. No matter how many descriptions of the Wiccan God I read, none of them resonated with me, and all I could think of was Jehovah with antlers, which didn't really inspire me all that much. It took years for these images to evolve into a Deity I could identify with, and only then could we start to build a relationship that wasn't based on so much baggage.

There is absolutely nothing wrong with Dianism, in my mind. I think there is room for all paths up this mountain, and to say any healing, ethical paths are "wrong" is to put blinders on to the glorious variety of human experience. However, if you have turned away from the traditional Wiccan model of balanced Divinity because of Jehovah, give the God a chance to show Himself in a kinder, more dynamic light. There are as many ways to be masculine as there are to be feminine, and either can transcend the bounds of physical anatomy and societal conditioning.

Men, I charge you: stand up and fill the gaps in Wiccan ritual with your own mysteries. Create your own image of what it means to be a man in our religion. Women can't do it for you any more than you could for us. Robe yourselves in the mantle of the God and step into the Circle where you belong—right beside the Goddess, in the light.

Concerning Initiation

Traditional Wiccans—which is to say the variety found primarily in Europe and primarily of Gardnerian lineage—place a good deal of emphasis on initiation into a coven as the only way to become a real Wiccan. American Wiccans, also known as "eclectic Wiccans," are often criticized for our build-your-own-trad-in-six-months approach. I have no intention of jumping into the ring on this argument, but as it happens, I agree with the spirit of the Traditional view, although not the literal meaning.

That is to say, you cannot be a Wiccan without having been initiated. However, what I mean by "initiation" isn't necessarily what a coven would mean. In fact, in using that word, I am not necessarily referring to a ritual at all.

The word *initiation* means "beginning." Whenever you embark on a new spiritual path, you are inviting change into your life. Often just after beginning, new and unforeseen challenges arise to help you prove your mettle, if only to yourself. There is no way to become a more spiritual person without change. This is doubly true for Wiccans, who mark their entry into the religion with a good deal of ceremony and significance.

For some Wiccans, the initiation ritual in and of itself doesn't constitute a real initiation. The real initiation—the bond with the Lord and Lady that makes a Wiccan what she is—may come later, gradually, and if she's lucky, quietly. Most often, however, after an initiation ritual, your life will fall apart in some way. Old, outmoded habits will have to be discarded, and you may be faced with the task of fashioning a new self out of the ashes of the old. Sometimes this happens gracefully without a lot of drama, but not often. You have to be prepared to face a sort of trial by fire of your way of looking at the world, yourself, and Deity.

This isn't meant to scare you out of initiating. In fact, if you want to be a Wiccan, as I said, you have to be initiated—but whether the ritual itself is handled by a group or by yourself is immaterial. Real initiation is between you and the gods. The change it brings about is a joyful thing, which will eventually transform you into the priest or priestess you truly are. Don't fear it; just be prepared. The God and Goddess won't throw anything at you that you can't handle. The most important lesson is that you *can* do it—you can change yourself, and therefore the world.

The upshot is, never take an initiation lightly. No matter how long you've studied or how secure you think you are, entering into an initiation is calling on the universe to start your life over. You are creating a space inside yourself for the God and Goddess, and it will be filled with change, discovery, and joy. Wicca is a religion of transformation, of one season giving way to the next. The serpent must shed its skin in order to grow. The Dance of Life goes on, and we have only to dance with it to find our path to Deity.

THREE THINGS TO THINK ON

1. Think of an event that is likely to happen to you, or one that already has, and plan a simple ritual for it. Where do you get stuck in the creative process—at the idea, the action, or the stuff? What resources could you use to help unblock you?

2. What kind of gender mysteries have you attended or been a part of? Did they have counterparts in the opposite gen-

der? If you are male, what rites of passage do you wish that young men growing up in Wicca could participate in?

3. Mentally go back in time to any initiations you have undergone, whether self-initiated or group initiated. Looking back, how did the initiation change you? What happened in your life afterward? If you are facing an impending initiation, what are you prepared to part with from your old life to make way for what is to come?

PART TWO

The Book of Moonlight

THE FOLLOWING PAGES ARE A sort of Devotional Book of Shadows—a series of rituals, prayers, and other useful information I have compiled for primarily solitary use. These texts are only examples of what this kind of Wicca can look and sound like. Try them as they are, change the wording, play with them until they feel right to you. Invocations and prayers written by someone else rarely have the feeling and intent you want them to, so I highly recommend reading through these and, with their spirit in mind, creating your own. (There's nothing worse than having to stop midway through an invocation and moan, "I can't believe she actually used the word 'effulgent'!") Blessed be.

Book Blessing

God and Goddess
Authors of the longest tale
Keepers of the eternal Dance

I ask Your blessing upon these pages
Live within me and within these words
Let them be a candle to lead me on Your path
As You will it, as I will it
With harm to none
With love for all
As it is written, so shall it be.
Blessed be.

A Pledge of Grace

I who am priest/ess of the God and Goddess do resolve
To open my heart to love in all its forms
To see with eyes of compassion
To act mindfully and with integrity
To see the humor in the joyous turnings of life
To have gratitude for the thousand blessings poured out upon me
To honor my own wisdom and that of others
To seek growth, to evolve, to learn.

A Morning Devotion

To be performed upon rising.

Tools: altar (set up as usual), a white candle, incense (if desired)

Light the candle and incense. Stand facing the altar, arms at your sides. Take a few deep breaths from down in your belly, grounding yourself gently through the cycles of your breath.

Turn to the east. Bring your arms up and out as if a cool wind is blowing through your fingers. Imagine the morning breeze, fresh and invigorating, opening your mind. Say:

Good morning, spirits of the East, creatures of Air.
Today with your blessing I walk the path of inspiration and
*   laughter.*
I follow the hawk on the ghost of the wind.
I find my voice and speak the truth.
Blessed be.

Face north, holding your arms out parallel to the ground, palms flat. Close your eyes and sense the stability and silence of the Earth beneath you. Call to the Earth, saying words such as:

Good morning, spirits of the North, creatures of Earth.
Today with your blessing I walk the path of strength and success.
I follow the steps of the wolf and bear.
Abundance grows all around me.
Blessed be.

Turn south. Hold your arms down, hands out as if you are warming yourself before a bonfire. Sense fire's healing warmth and power. Say:

Good morning, spirits of the South, creatures of Fire.
Today with your blessing I walk the path of passion and courage.
I follow the snake through the silver desert.

I *create change with the flame of my will.*
Blessed be.

Turn to the west. Curve your arms into a circle, as though they hold an ocean within them. Sense the rise and fall of the tide. Say:

Good morning, spirits of the West, creatures of Water.
Today with your blessing I walk the path of beauty and love.
I follow the dolphin into the hidden depths.
My blood is the healing blood of the sea.
Blessed be.

Return to the altar. Stand first in the traditional God position, arms crossed over your chest. Bring your arms up into Goddess position (arms upraised in a V-shape). Close your eyes and feel the love of God and Goddess poured out upon you. Say:

Good morning Lord and Lady.
Today with Your blessing I walk with You
Upon a path of my own choosing.
Guide and guard me this day and always.
By your grace, with harm to none,
Blessed be.

When you feel calm, strong, and ready to go about your day, extinguish the candle.

An Evening Devotion

To be performed before retiring.

Tools: same as for the morning devotion

Light your candle and incense. Take a moment to reflect on the day just past—on the many decisions, successes, and experiences that made the day what it was, for better or worse. Let these events become the past, as tomorrow is a new day, a new chance.

Beginning in the west, give thanks to each element for the gifts you received this day, using the same gestures as in the morning devotion. Suggested words are as follows:

Good evening, spirits of the West, creatures of Water
I thank you for the compassion you have given me
This and every day.
Grant me peaceful dreams tonight
That I may stand in your tide again tomorrow.
Blessed be.
Good evening, spirits of the North, creatures of Earth
I thank you for the balance you have given me
This and every day.
Grant me sound sleep tonight
That I may walk with you tomorrow.
Blessed be.
Good evening, spirits of the East, creatures of Air
I thank you for the wisdom you have given me
This and every day.

Grant me dreams with wings tonight
That I may rise renewed with you tomorrow.
Blessed be.
Good evening, spirits of the South, creatures of Fire
I thank you for the energy you have given me
This and every day.
Grant me your protective warmth as I sleep
That I may dance with you again tomorrow.
Blessed be.

Return to the altar and perform the God and Goddess gestures as in the morning devotion.

Good evening Lord and Lady
I thank You for the life You have given me to weave
This and every day.
I pray that You will watch over my sleep tonight
That I may keep well to Your path tomorrow.
By Your grace, with harm to none,
Blessed be.

Allow the radiance of Deity to fill you with quiet and peace. When you are centered, relaxed, and ready to sleep, extinguish the candle.

An Attunement and Self-Blessing

Based on the chakra system.

Use this brief meditation to help ground and center yourself in times of duress.

Take several deep breaths to calm your mind. Continue to breathe deeply as you speak or think the words that follow, visualizing Divine energy flowing up your body, higher with each inhalation.

Beginning with the crown chakra, just above the top of the head:

Bless me, Lord and Lady, for I am Your child and am part of You.

Then to the third eye:

Bless my vision with the light of wisdom.

Then to the throat:

Bless my voice with truth and integrity.

Then to the heart:

Bless my heart with perfect love.

Then the solar plexus:

Bless my will with strength of purpose.

Then the belly:

> *Bless my passions with balance.*

Then the root chakra, at the base of the spine:

> *Bless my instincts with clarity.*

The soles of the feet:

> *Bless the path I walk with honor and beauty.*

The palms of the hands:

> *Bless my hands that they may do Your work on this Earth.*

Returning to the crown:

> *Bless me, Lord and Lady, for I am Your child and am part of You.*

An Offering Rite

To be performed outdoors near a body of water, preferably a flowing one.

This short ritual expresses gratitude for a particular gift you have received or something you have accomplished with the Lord and Lady's help. You can either offer your thanks, or symbolically "give" Them your accomplishment by sending it into the water. Have with you either a handful of some kind of seed native to your area (so not to disturb the local ecosystem with foreign plants) or a leaf on which you have written what you are grateful for.

Hold the offering in both hands and lift it to the sky, saying:

By the ever-flowing stream
and the endless blue sky,
I give thanks for your blessings, Mother and Father
and offer you my love and devotion.
Blessed be.

Now gently cast your offering into the water and watch it as it is carried away.

Lunar Celebratory Rituals

This first ritual should be performed on the night of the full moon, in view of the moon if possible. If not, light a white candle to represent her energy. Prepare for the ritual in your usual way; you may want to keep a special garment aside for celebratory or lunar rites.

Declare sacred space in your usual way.

Light your candle and face the altar, or stand in view of the moon herself. If you are unable to see her, envision her in all her cool radiance in the sky above. Stand in the Goddess position, letting the light of the moon flow down into you, filling you with peace, love, and strength.

Invoke the Goddess silently or aloud with words such as:

Lady of light,
Mother of All,
Queen of the farthest stars,
You call me forth from the waking world
And gladly I come
To stand before You beneath the velvet black of night
I seek Your mystery, the light within
Great Mother, Star-Eyed Wonder,
On this night edged in silver
As in every moment
I reach for Your hand.

Now celebrate the Goddess in whatever way feels appropriate: dance, chant, sing, play music, meditate, or simply share a chalice with the Lady and spend a while in communion with Her. Be open to any counsel She has for you, and tell Her anything that needs to be said.

To close the ritual, just before thanking the elements, say words such as:

Great Mother of all things
As I have partaken of Your compassion
this full moon's night
So may I take You with me through the days
and bestow upon all creatures
that which You give me
Unquestionably, without condition or limit.
Star of the Sea

Bright Lady, Radiant One
I am, as always, in Your service.
Blessed be.

On the dark of the moon, a similar rite may be performed in an unlit room in honor of the Dark Mother who lives within the still, quiet reaches of the soul. Use an invocation like the following:

Dark Mother
Whose hand guides the dance of life and death
Patient weaver of the silver web
I hear Your call from the pause between breaths
And as I have sought You outside
Tonight I seek you in.
Teach me of the deepest sea
Of the wild hunt and the mourning cry
Tonight in the darkness
Which bears the seeds of daybreak
I reach for Your hand.

Meditate on the month gone by, the month ahead, and what the Dark Mother has taught you. Listen deep within yourself for Her voice. To close the ritual, bid farewell with such words as:

Ancient Mother
Creator and Destroyer

As I have partaken of Your wisdom
This dark moon's night
So may I take that wisdom with me into the day
and remember that every ending is a beginning
and all that falls shall rise again.
Star of the Sea,
Darkest Abyss,
I am, as always, in Your service.
Blessed be.

Solar Celebratory Ritual

To be performed during daylight, either in view of the sun or in a room bathed in his light.

Prepare for ritual and declare sacred space in your usual way.

Stand either before your altar or in the sunlight, holding your arms crossed over your chest in God position. Feel the healing warmth of the sun filling you, flooding your heart with radiant joy. Invoke the God silently, or with the following words:

Father, Sun, and Brother
Who wears a cloak of bright blue sky
Whose breath stirs the forest
Whose love draws the harvest from the soil
I hear Your call in the wolf's song
Teach me the holiness of joy, the sanctity of living.
I join You on the hillside

To dance in Your light
To reach for Your hand.

As in the lunar rituals, create a celebratory action that reflects your connection to the God. Spend time with Him, listening for His voice shining through your window. When you are ready to close the ritual, bid farewell in a manner like the following:

Lord of all the wildlands
Warrior and poet, the rising grain and the shining blade,
As I have partaken of Your strength and surety
So may I carry them with me
And share Your blessings with all the world.
Father of the Daybreak,
Divine Friend,
I am, as always, in Your service.
Blessed be.

Dedication/Affirmation Ritual

Begin the ritual in silence and in darkness, with only the light of a single white candle to guide you. This candle represents you, your life up to this point: all your successes, failures, joys, and heartaches. It also represents your spiritual history even as far back as childhood; we have all been shaped by the beliefs of our youth.

Bathe in warm water, with your candle lit nearby. Use this time to cleanse yourself of your worries, of your expectations for the coming rite. You come before the gods with a loving heart—all will be well.

When you rise from the bath, anoint yourself with an oil that has meaning to you personally, or use something like sandalwood or rosemary. Dab it on your wrists, third eye, and heart. Remember that you are robing yourself as a priestess and that, as a priestess, your every action is one of reverence.

Holding your candle, make your way to the place where you have set up your altar. Before you should be two taper candles representing the God and Goddess of whatever colors that symbolize Their energy to you. Also, have between them a large white candle that will serve henceforth as your devotional candle to symbolize your commitment to Divine mystery.

Hold your candle aloft as you call to the elements either silently or using words such as the following:

I call to the silent Earth
The ground beneath my feet
I call to the shadowed mountain and the towering redwood
Guide me down the less-trodden path
Come, if you will, to my Circle tonight.
Hail and welcome.
I call to the wandering Air
The wind at my back
I call to the leaf-strewn breeze and the cool of morning
Teach me to speak the truth without fear
Come, if you will, to my Circle tonight.

Hail and welcome.
I call to the dancing Fire
The spark that drives my heartbeat
I call to the sun-stripped desert and the summer lightning
Inspire me to live my true passions
Come, if you will, to my Circle tonight.
Hail and welcome.
I call to the drifting Water
The tears and sweat I have shed
I call to the lowering thundercloud and the crystalline falls
Show me the depths of love and healing
Come, if you will, to my Circle tonight.
Hail and welcome.

Light the candle on your altar that symbolizes the God, using the candle in your hand. Invoke the God as you wish; suggested words follow. Then repeat the procedure for the Goddess candle.

God of the Sun and all its blessings
God of the ancient groves
Father, I who am Your [son/daughter] call You
I call Your strength from the oak
I call Your wisdom from the mountain
I call Your love from within and all around me.
Father of a thousand names,
Ever living, ever dying,

Come, if you will, to my Circle tonight.

Hail and welcome.

Goddess of the Moon and all its blessings

Goddess of the restless sea

Mother, I who am Your [son/daughter] call You

I call Your peace from the shining lake

I call Your power from the standing stones

I call Your love from within and all around me

Mother with a thousand voices

Ever waxing, ever waning

Come, if you will, to my Circle tonight.

Hail and welcome.

Return to your altar and, for a moment, contemplate the candle you have been holding. Trace in your memory the many events that have brought you to this time, this moment, this commitment. Even the worst day in your life had its place in getting you here.

You have lit the flames of the future with your past, and you can embrace the lessons and let go of the pain. Now, decisively, extinguish your candle.

This is the time to make whatever vows you have come before the gods to make. Do not promise anything that in your heart you know you will not try to follow through on. You might use something like "A Pledge of Grace" in earlier pages, or if there are specific goals you have as a dedicant to your path or have for the coming year, incorporate those. It may be helpful to write your vow out on paper and keep it in a box or other vessel on your altar. Then burn the old each year to make way for the new. Here is a very simple example:

> *In the presence of the Mother and Father of all things*
> *By the sanctity of Earth, Water, Fire, and Air*
> *By my honor as Wiccan and [priest/priestess]*
> *I vow this night to serve the God and Goddess*
> *To be an agent of Their love and kindness*
> *To learn and grow in spirit*
> *By Their grace, and with harm to none,*
> *So mote it be.*

Take up both the God and Goddess candles, and use their flames together to light your devotional candle. If you feel more words are appropriate, by all means say them. If not, spend a while in silence and meditate on the path you have chosen and how this choice will influence your life.

Because the goal of this ritual is to show your desire for unity with the Divine, you may not wish to bid farewell to the energies you have called, preferring to encourage them to remain with you. If you feel more comfortable releasing the Circle as is traditional, feel free to do so. Otherwise close the ritual with an expression of gratitude such as:

> *I give thanks, Lord and Lady, for Your presence here*
> *And for Your continued blessings.*
> *I give thanks to the Earth, Air, Fire, and Water all around,*
> *Who are also a part of me.*

Walk with me and abide in my steps, now and always.
Blessed be.

Building and Consecrating Your Temple

Before performing this ritual, clean your home from top to bottom. As you do so, visualize all the past impressions and negative energy that may have built up being washed away, leaving a clean space for you to build your temple in. Take special care to clean your altar; or, if you don't already have one, set it up. Finally, cleanse yourself in a bath or shower and dress for the ritual.

You will need an object or picture to represent each of the four elements. Be sure to decide beforehand on a location for each of them around the house. (A compass would come in handy here.) Also have a bowl or other receptacle with herbs, grain, or some other offering to the nature spirits and other creatures who inhabit the land your home is built upon.

The invocations for this rite will depend entirely on the image you have chosen for your hearth temple, as in chapter 4. Craft your words based upon that image.

As an example, suppose you wanted your home to have the gentle, supportive energy of a forest grove. Your ritual could, perhaps, flow as follows: walk slowly counterclockwise around your home, sprinkling salted water as you go. The water cleanses the last vestiges of negative influence, preparing the space. Repeat softly to yourself, "By Earth and Water I cleanse this space."

Choose an incense that reminds you of the environment you wish to foster. In this example pine, cedar, sage, or any other woody scent would be appropriate. Carry the incense around the house, letting its smoke drift into each corner. Don't forget bathrooms, closets, the garage, and so forth. Visualize the smoke creating a soft barrier, a division between your home and the outside world. Repeat as you walk, "By Fire and Air I consecrate this space."

Next, take up each elemental object in turn and invoke that element. When you have called the element, visualize it in whatever way your invocation suggests, filling your home with its presence and protection. Then take the object you have chosen and place it in that direction, saying, "Hail and welcome."

Example invocations:

In this sacred grove, I call the oak
I call the birch and pine and ash
I call the ivy winding toward the sun
I call the stones and soil
Earth, my strength, my abundance, I call you.
In this sacred grove, I call the wind
I call the turning starlit sky
I call the birdsong, the drifting leaves
I call the stillness of a spring evening
Air, my humor, my song, I call you.
In this sacred grove, I call the sun
I call the leaping bonfire

I call the warmth of a summer afternoon
I call the flash of distant lightning
Fire, my power, my passion, I call you.
In this sacred grove, I call the river
I call the scent of wild roses
I call the dew, the mist, the downpour
I call the rain's renewal.
Water, my healing, my peace, I call you.

Now spend time exploring your grove, strengthening the visualization until it is completely real to you. Imagine the sounds around you, the temperature and scent, the feel of the earth beneath your feet. See the image of your chosen temple superimposed over your mundane home, infusing each brick with the energies you have called. If you like a more formal energy-raising, chant or dance around the space, channeling the energy into the walls and furnishings.

When the vision is as strong as you can make it and you are ready to proceed, return to your altar, the cornerstone of your temple. Again, your invocations to the Lord and Lady will depend on the nature of your vision, but to follow the grove example: light your devotional candle if you haven't already, as well as any candles you have representing Divine presence.

Great Mother and Father
I stand here in my home, my temple, my sacred grove
Surrounded by Your children

I, Your child, invite You to this place.
Though You never leave me,
My door is always open to You
Live in my heart and I in Yours
I dedicate this grove in Your honor
As a sanctuary of Your mysteries
As a dwelling place for perfect love and trust.
As I will it
By Your grace, and with harm to none,
Blessed be.

As this ritual creates a permanent Circle in your home, you will not open it. You may wish to close the rite, however, with a few words, or simply extinguish your candles and consider the temple completed.

On a monthly basis, or however often you feel it necessary, perform a short rite to recleanse and strengthen your temple's perimeter. Smudge the house with the same or similar incense as before, and spend time visualizing in the same manner, adding whatever energy seems needed. Use words if the desire moves you.

Prayers, Affirmations, and Blessings

A Morning Prayer

Good morning, God and Goddess
I rise today with gratitude
For the twenty-four new hours You have given me.

Help me to live them with wisdom and courage
Help me to come from a place of love for all
Let me face joy and sorrow, virtue and vice
With a strong heart and a clear mind.
Blessed be.

AN EVENING PRAYER

Good evening, God and Goddess
I give thanks for this day in all its richness
and for the lessons I have learned.
Thank You for walking beside me
Thank You for bringing me safely to rest.
Bless this night with peaceful dreams
Watch over me, Mother and Father, now and always.
Blessed be.

A MEAL BLESSING

Lord and Lady
I give thanks for this meal
and for the plants, animals, and people
who gave their lives and labor that I might enjoy it.
May it nourish me in body, mind, and spirit.
By Your grace, with harm to none,
Blessed be.

A PRAYER FOR THE DAILY COMMUTE

Gracious Mother and Father
Guide my way to [work/home] today

See me safely to my destination
Keep my thoughts clear and calm
And my [vehicle] in good working order
By Your grace do I depart
By Your grace will I arrive.
Blessed be.

A PRAYER FOR SAFE TRAVEL

God and Goddess bless this journey
Let it be free of mishaps of all kinds
Let me reach my destination safely
And let time spent at journey's end
Be well worth the trip.
By Your grace do I depart
By Your grace will I arrive
Blessed be.

A BLESSING ON A HOME

Great Mother of the Earth and Sea
Great Father of the Wooded Wildlands
I ask Your protection on my home
and on all that dwells within its walls.
Hold it securely in Your arms
Safe from intrusion and disaster
Let it be a sanctuary of Your compassion
to nourish all who enter in perfect love and trust.
Blessed be.

A PRAYER BEFORE WORK

I am Your priestess, Mother and Father
Let this work be a sacrament
As I support my livelihood
May my actions be a prayer
May my hands and words be balanced
May I walk with Your grace.
With harm to none, and love for all,
So mote it be.

A PRAYER BEFORE COOKING

Earth and Water, Fire and Air
Love and joy and laughter
All come together in this food.
I nurture others and I am nurtured by Your love.
Goddess of the verdant Earth,
God of the ripening harvest,
Bless the stirring of this spoon,
Bless the stirring of our hearts.
Blessed be.

A MEAL BLESSING FOR A GROUP

Blessed are all who gather here
Blessed is the bounty we share
Blessed are those who are not with us to share it
Nourished are we by this feast
Nourished are we by each other

Nourished are we by our Mother and Father.
Blessed be.

A Prayer for Protection

These woods are dark
This path is shadowed
Walk with me, Lord and Lady
Hunter of the Forests, stand at my back
Star-Eyed Protectress, fold Your wings around me
Hold me fast, I pray
and banish all fear.
With harm to none,
So mote it be.

A Prayer for Solace

The Moon to my left, the Sun to my right
Your love all around me
My aching heart grows stronger
I will emerge from this darkness and breathe again.
Blessed Mother, help me through
Blessed Father, help me through
[repeat last two lines as necessary]

A Prayer for Guidance and Clarity

The path lies before me overgrown
tangled with doubts and indecision
Help me, Great Mother, I pray
Help me find my way through the forest.

Lord of the greenwood, guide my steps
Breathe clarity into my sight
If I should fall, help me to rise.
Blessed be.

A Prayer for Assistance in Dealing with Difficult People

Thou art Goddess
Thou art God
I greet you from a place of love
I will honor us both
We breathe the same air,
Feel the same pains,
Do our best with what we know.
I will honor us both.
Thou art Goddess
Thou art God
As am I, as are we all.

An Affirmation

My Mother brought me forth
and I am She.
I see with Her eyes,
I sing with Her mouth,
I dream with Her mind,
I work with Her hands,
I create with Her womb,

I dance with Her feet,
I love with Her heart,
I hold the world in Her arms,
I rejoice in Her spirit.
I am Her perfect child
I am held safe in Her embrace.

A Prayer of Thanks

When I felt there was no hope
I saw Your love in the eyes of a friend
When I had no joy
I heard Your laughter in the wind
When my heart was full of dust
I bathed in Your light and was renewed
When I was a frightened little girl
You held me safe in the circle of Your arms
Blessings, Mother, for Your love and strength
May I never forget You live within me.

Recomme[...]
and Bibliog[...]

Berthold-Bond, Annie. *Clean and Green: The Complete Guide to Non-Toxic and Environmentally Safe Housekeeping.* Woodstock, N.Y.: Ceres Press, 1994.

An excellent book with dozens of great ideas.

Cunningham, Scott. *Living Wicca.* St. Paul, Minn.: Llewellyn, 1993.

Sequel to Wicca: A Guide for the Solitary Practitioner, with information on creating your own tradition.

————. *Wicca: A Guide for the Solitary Practitioner.* St. Paul, Minn.: Llewellyn, 1990.

The absolutely indispensable handbook for the beginning solitary.

*hyllis. Book of Shadows: A Modern Woman's Journey
ne Wisdom of Witchcraft and the Magic of the Goddess.
w York: Broadway Books, 1999.

Part guide and part autobiography; poetic and intensely spiritual.

————. *Witch Crafting.* New York: Broadway Books, 2001.

*A truly beautiful work on spiritual magic by a truly amazing
witch—giving Scott Cunningham a serious run for his money.*

Farrington, Debra. *Living Faith Day by Day: How the Sacred
Rules of Monastic Traditions Can Help You Live Spiritually in
the Modern World.* New York: Perigee, 2000.

*A guide to fitting the principles of a monastic life into life in
the wider world.*

Fisher, Amber Laine. *Philosophy of Wicca.* Toronto, Canada:
ECW Press, 2002.

*A deep and insightful exploration of the meanings behind Wic-
can beliefs and practices.*

Galenorn, Yasmine. *Embracing the Moon: A Witch's Guide to
Rituals, Spellcraft, and Shadow Work.* St. Paul, Minn.:
Llewellyn, 1998.

*Yasmine does not call herself a Wiccan, but her books are a fab-
ulous resource for Wiccan and non-Wiccan alike.*

Hutton, Ronald. *The Triumph of the Moon: A History of Modern Pagan Witchcraft.* New York: Oxford University Press, 1999.

At last, a scholarly history of the Craft movement, well researched and thought provoking.

Johnson, Cait. *Cooking Like a Goddess: Bringing Seasonal Magic into the Kitchen.* Rochester, Vt.: Healing Arts Press, 1997.

Not just a cookbook, this is a handbook for treating the kitchen as sacred space.

Johnson, Cait, and Maura D. Shaw. *Celebrating the Great Mother: A Handbook of Earth-Honoring Activities for Parents and Children.* Rochester, Vt.: Destiny Books, 1995.

Great fun for kids and adults, with heaps of ideas for the sabbats.

Judith, Anodea. *Wheels of Life: A User's Guide to the Chakra System.* St. Paul, Minn.: Llewellyn, 1999.

Engaging, exhaustive tome. Don't let its length intimidate you—there's something good on every page.

Moran, Victoria. *Shelter for the Spirit: Create Your Own Haven in a Hectic World.* New York: HarperPerennial, 1998.

Lovely, lovely book. A must-have for anyone with a hearth-based trad.

Muten, Burleigh, ed. *Her Words: An Anthology of Poetry About the Great Goddess.* Boston: Shambhala Publications, 1999.

Ancient and modern writing in Her honor, with a number of invocations suitable for ritual use.

Nhat Hanh, Thich. *Peace Is Every Step: The Path of Mindfulness in Everyday Life.* New York: Bantam, 1992.

A beautiful, gentle book on an essential practice.

Orr, Emma Restall. *Ritual: A Guide to Life, Love and Inspiration.* London: Thorsons, 2000.

A look at creating ritual from a modern Druid perspective.

Reed, Ellen Cannon. *The Heart of Wicca: Wise Words from a Crone on the Path.* York Beach, Maine: Samuel Weiser, 2000.

The first book I've seen questioning the trends of pop Wicca.

Roberts, Elizabeth, and Elias Amidon, eds. *Earth Prayers from Around the World.* San Francisco: HarperSanFrancisco, 1991.

They're not kidding—hundreds of prayers to a wide variety of Deities, many from familiar faces.

Roth, Gabrielle. *Sweat Your Prayers: Movement as Spiritual Practice*. New York: Putnam, 1997.

This book is a dance in itself, covering Gabrielle's Five Rhythms system of ecstatic movement.

Sewell, Marilyn, ed. *Cries of the Spirit: A Celebration of Women's Spirituality*. Boston: Beacon, 1991.

Another book of poems, invocations, and prayers in many traditions.

Starhawk. *The Spiral Dance: A Rebirth of the Ancient Religion of the Great Goddess*. 20th anniversary ed. San Francisco: Harper San Francisco, 2000.

Usually one of the first books new Pagans pick up, and a beautiful work of poetic theology.

Starhawk, with Hilary Valentine. *The Twelve Wild Swans: Rituals, Exercises & Magical Training in the Reclaiming Tradition*. San Francisco: Harper San Francisco, 2000.

Finally, a book that goes beyond the basics!

Walsh, Roger. *Essential Spirituality: The 7 Central Practices to Awaken Heart and Mind*. New York: John Wiley and Sons, 2000.

Explores the wisdom of six of the major religions to help us live spiritually in a material society.

Index

☽ ORDER LLEWELLYN BOOKS TODAY!

Llewellyn publishes hundreds of books on your favorite
subjects! To get these exciting books, including the ones on the following
pages, check your local bookstore or order them directly from Llewellyn.

Order Online:
Visit our website at www.llewellyn.com, select your books, and order
them on our secure server.

Order by Phone:
- Call toll-free within the U.S. at 1-877-NEW-WRLD (1-877-639-9753). Call toll-free within Canada at 1-866-NEW-WRLD (1-866-639-9753)
- We accept VISA, MasterCard, and American Express

Order by Mail:
Send the full price of your order (MN residents add 7% sales tax) in
U.S. funds, plus postage & handling to:
> **Llewellyn Worldwide**
> **P.O. Box 64383, Dept. 0-7387-0348-6**
> **St. Paul, MN 55164-0383, U.S.A.**

Postage & Handling:
> **Standard** (U.S., Mexico, & Canada). If your order is:
> > Up to $25.00, add $3.50
> > $25.01 - $48.99, add $4.00
> > $49.00 and over, FREE STANDARD SHIPPING
>
> (Continental U.S. orders ship UPS. AK, HI, PR, & P.O. Boxes
> ship USPS 1st class. Mex. & Can. ship PMB.)

> **International Orders:**
> > **Surface Mail:** For orders of $20.00 or less, add $5 plus
> > $1 per item ordered. For orders of $20.01 and over,
> > add $6 plus $1 per item ordered.
>
> > **Air Mail:**
> > *Books:* Postage & Handling is equal to the total retail
> > price of all books in the order.
> > *Non-book items:* Add $5 for each item.

Orders are processed within 2 business days. Please allow for normal
shipping time. Postage and handling rates subject to change.

Wicca

A Guide for the Solitary Practitioner

SCOTT CUNNINGHAM

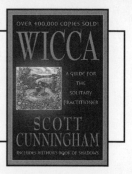

Wicca is a book of life, and how to live magically, spiritually, and wholly attuned with Nature. It is a book of sense and common sense, not only about Magick, but about religion and one of the most critical issues of today: how to achieve the much needed and wholesome relationship with our Earth. Cunningham presents Wicca as it is today: a gentle, Earth-oriented religion dedicated to the Goddess and God. This book fulfills a need for a practical guide to solitary Wicca—a need that no previous book has fulfilled.

This book presents the theory and practice of Wicca from an individual's perspective. The section on the Standing Stones Book of Shadows contains solitary rituals for the Esbats and Sabbats. This book, based on the author's nearly two decades of Wiccan practice, presents an eclectic picture of various aspects of this religion.

0-87542-118-0
240 pp., 6 x 9, illus. $9.95

Spanish edition:
Wicca: Una guía para la práctica individual
0-7387-0306-0 $14.95

To order, call 1-877-NEW-WRLD
Prices subject to change without notice

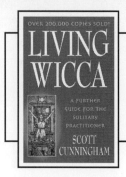

Living Wicca

A *Further Guide for the*
Solitary Practitioner

SCOTT CUNNINGHAM

Living Wicca is the long-awaited sequel to Scott Cunningham's wildly successful *Wicca: A Guide for the Solitary Practitioner*. This book is for those who have made the conscious decision to bring their Wiccan spirituality into their everyday lives. It provides solitary practitioners with the tools and added insights that will enable them to blaze their own spiritual paths—to become their own high priests and priestesses.

Living Wicca takes a philosophical look at the questions, practices, and differences within Witchcraft. It covers the various tools of learning available to the practitioner, the importance of secrecy in one's practice, guidelines to performing ritual when ill, magical names, initiation, and the Mysteries. It discusses the benefits of daily prayer and meditation, making offerings to the gods, how to develop a prayerful attitude, and how to perform Wiccan rites when away from home or in emergency situations.

0-87542-184-9
208 pp., 6 x 9, illus. $12.95

To order, call 1-877-NEW-WRLD
Prices subject to change without notice

Embracing the Moon

A Witch's Guide to Rituals, Spellcraft & Shadow Work

YASMINE GALENORN

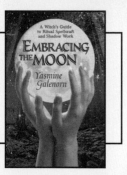

Do you feel like toasting the Gods with a glass of mead as you revel in the joys of life? Ever wish you could creep through the mists at night, hunting the Wild Lord? *Embracing the Moon* takes you into the core of Witchcraft, helping you weave magic into your daily routine. The spells and rituals are designed to give you the flexibility to experiment so that you are not locked into dogmatic, rigid degree-systems. Written to encompass both beginning and advanced practitioners, *Embracing the Moon* explores the mystical side of natural magic while keeping a commonsense attitude.

Packed not only with spells and rituals, but recipes for oils, spell powders, and charms, this book is based on personal experience; the author dots the pages with her own stories and anecdotes to give you fascinating, and sometimes humorous, examples of what you might expect out of working with her system of magic.

1-56718-304-2
312 pp., 6 x 9, illus. $14.95

Book of Hours

Prayers to the Goddess

GALEN GILLOTTE

Here is a book that moves beyond the conscious mind and into the heart and spirit. It is not about theory, techniques of ritual, or even of "practice." It is, simply, a book of Goddess-centered prayers, meditations, and affirmations. It includes morning, evening, and nightly prayers; seasonal prayers (for the Wiccan holy days); and prayers for the new and full moons.

Prayer is, essentially, speaking with Deity, but many people are confused about how to do this. This book will unveil the confusion. It is written for young and old, for the neophyte as well as the accomplished priest or priestess. It may be used in Wiccan circles, study groups, or anytime you want to connect to the Goddess. Ultimately, it is for those who have a deep hunger for that spiritual connection.

1-56718-273-9
168 pp., 5³⁄₁₆ x 8, hardcover $14.95

In the Circle

Crafting the Witches' Path

ELEN HAWKE

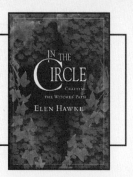

Are you new to witchcraft, or are you looking for fresh ideas to enliven your practice? Whatever your age or level of experience, this book is for you. Take a step-by-step journey through the Moon's phases, the eight seasonal festivals, an understanding of Goddess and God, building a shrine, collecting or making magical tools, performing ritual, exploring sacred sites, and many other aspects of modern witchcraft.

Containing nearly thirty of the author's own beautiful illustrations, In The Circle combines Elen Hawke's personal accounts of sabbats and Moon rites with a clear, commonsense approach that makes witchcraft accessible to anyone. Whether you want to practice alone, with a partner, or in a group, In the Circle will be a wise guide, providing answers that are inspirational and empowering. Each section takes you deeper into your inner core, the place where you can connect to the spirit of Nature and to your innate knowledge.

1-56718-444-8
192 pp., 6 x 9, illus. $12.95

To order, call 1-877-NEW-WRLD
Prices subject to change without notice

The Inner Temple of Witchcraft

Magick, Meditation &
Psychic Development

CHRISTOPHER PENCZAK

For the serious seeker, *The Inner Temple of Witchcraft* lays the foundation for deep experience with ritual. Instead of diving right into spellwork, this book sets the student on a course of experience with energy and psychic ability—the cornerstones of magick. You will explore witchcraft's ancient history and modern traditions, discovering the path that suits you best. The thirteen lessons take the student through meditation, instant magic, ancient philosophy, modern science, protection, light, energy anatomy, astral travel, spirit guides, and healing, culminating in a self-initiation ritual.

0-7387-0276-5
352 pp., 7½ x 9⅛ $17.95

To order, call 1-877-NEW-WRLD
Prices subject to change without notice

The Urban Primitive

Paganism in the Concrete Jungle

RAVEN KALDERA
AND TANNIN SCHWARTZSTEIN

Modern neo-paganism is primarily an urban movement, yet few books exist for city pagans, specifically city pagans on a budget. *The Urban Primitive* shows how every disaffected urban pagan can use magick to survive and make good in the city.

Find practical recommendations not found anywhere else, including how to protect your back in the combat zone, defend your house from intruders and lousy energies, find jobs, keep your car running, locate good parking spaces, and use the city's energy for sorcery. There are even chapters on body decoration, urban totem animals such as sparrows and cockroaches, and old gods in new guises including Skor (goddess of dumpster treasures) and Slick (god of fast talking).

0-7387-0259-5
264 pp., 6 x 9, illus. $14.95

Wheels of Life
A User's Guide to the Chakra System

ANODEA JUDITH

An instruction manual for owning and operating the inner gears that run the machinery of our lives. Written in a practical, down-to-earth style, this fully illustrated book will take the reader on a journey through aspects of consciousness, from the bodily instincts of survival to the processing of deep thoughts.

Discover this ancient metaphysical system under the new light of popular Western metaphors: quantum physics, Kabbalah, physical exercises, poetic meditations, and visionary art. Learn how to open these centers in yourself, and see how the chakras shed light on the present world crises we face today. And learn what you can do about it!

This book will be a vital resource for: magicians, witches, pagans, mystics, yoga practitioners, martial arts people, psychologists, medical people, and all those who are concerned with holistic growth techniques.

0-87542-320-5
528 pp., 6 x 9, illus. $17.95

To order, call 1-877-NEW-WRLD
Prices subject to change without notice

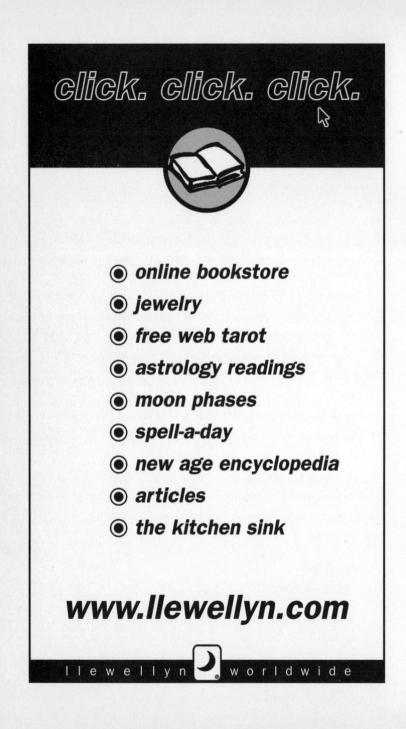